Short Cut Cookbook

Short Cut
Cookbook

Katie Stewart

HAMLYN
London · New York · Sydney · Toronto

The author and publisher would like to thank the following for their
co-operation in supplying colour photographs for this book
American Long Grain Rice 75
Birds Eye Foods Limited 35, 58
Buxted Advisory Service 45
Colman's Mustard 57
Dutch Dairy Bureau 93, 94
McDougalls Home Baking Bureau 18
Pasta Information Centre 76
Tea Council 111

Photography by Vic Paris of Alphaplus Studios, Leatherhead
Line drawings by Patricia Ludlow
Props kindly supplied by Ashton House, Hampton Hill, Middlesex

Published by
The Hamlyn Publishing Group Limited
London · New York · Sydney · Toronto
Astronaut House, Feltham, Middlesex, England
© Copyright The Hamlyn Publishing Group Limited 1979
Reprinted 1984

ISBN 0 600 31991 1

Printed in Italy

CONTENTS

Introduction

There are moments in every busy woman's life when the time available for preparing a meal is limited. This calls for quick thinking, good planning and plenty of imagination. It depends on using quick methods of cooking, a sensibly stocked larder and the best use of canned, packet and frozen foods. In fact, short-cut cooking means not so much cooking with less time involved, but rather working so that you plan, buy or cook when you have got the time, in order to make it easier when you haven't.

Katie Stewart.

Useful facts and figures

Notes on metrication
In this book quantities are given in metric and Imperial measures. Exact conversion from Imperial to metric measures does not usually give very convenient working quantities and so the metric measures have been rounded off into units of 25 grams. The table below shows the recommended equivalents.

Ounces	Approx g to nearest whole figure	Recom-mended conversion to nearest unit of 25	Ounces	Approx g to nearest whole figure	Recom-mended conversion to nearest unit of 25
1	28	25	11	312	300
2	57	50	12	340	350
3	85	75	13	368	375
4	113	100	14	396	400
5	142	150	15	425	425
6	170	175	16 (1 lb)	454	450
7	198	200	17	482	475
8	227	225	18	510	500
9	255	250	19	539	550
10	283	275	20 (1¼ lb)	567	575

Note: When converting quantities over 20 oz first add the appropriate figures in the centre column, then adjust to the nearest unit of 25. As a general guide, 1 kg (1000 g) equals 2·2 lb or about 2 lb 3 oz. This method of conversion gives good results in nearly all cases, although in certain pastry and cake recipes a more accurate conversion is necessary to produce a balanced recipe.

Liquid measures The millilitre has been used in this book and the following table gives a few examples.

Imperial	Approx ml to nearest whole figure	Recom-mended ml	Imperial	Approx ml to nearest whole figure	Recom-mended ml
¼ pint	142	150 ml	1 pint	567	600 ml
½ pint	283	300 ml	1½ pints	851	900 ml
¾ pint	425	450 ml	1¾ pints	992	1000 ml (1 litre)

Spoon measures All spoon measures given in this book are level unless otherwise stated.

Can sizes At present, cans are marked with the exact (usually to the nearest whole number) metric equivalent of the Imperial weight of the contents, so we have followed this practice when giving can sizes.

Oven temperatures

The table below gives recommended equivalents.

	°C	°F	Gas Mark		°C	°F	Gas Mark
Very cool	110	225	$\frac{1}{4}$	Moderately hot	190	375	5
	120	250	$\frac{1}{2}$		200	400	6
Cool	140	275	1	Hot	220	425	7
	150	300	2		230	450	8
Moderate	160	325	3	Very hot	240	475	9
	180	350	4				

Notes for American and Australian users

In America the 8-oz measuring cup is used. In Australia metric measures are now used in conjunction with the standard 250-ml measuring cup. The Imperial pint, used in Britain and Australia, is 20 fl oz, while the American pint is 16 fl oz. It is important to remember that the Australian tablespoon differs from both the British and American tablespoons; the table below gives a comparison. The British standard tablespoon, which has been used throughout this book, holds 17·7 ml, the American 14·2 ml, and the Australian 20 ml. A teaspoon holds approximately 5 ml in all three countries.

British	American	Australian	British	American	Australian
1 teaspoon	1 teaspoon	1 teaspoon	$3\frac{1}{2}$ tablespoons	4 tablespoons	3 tablespoons
1 tablespoon	1 tablespoon	1 tablespoon	4 tablespoons	5 tablespoons	$3\frac{1}{2}$ tablespoons
2 tablespoons	3 tablespoons	2 tablespoons			

An Imperial/American guide to solid and liquid measures

IMPERIAL	AMERICAN	IMPERIAL	AMERICAN
1 lb butter or margarine	2 cups	$\frac{1}{4}$ pint liquid	$\frac{2}{3}$ cup liquid
		$\frac{1}{2}$ pint	$1\frac{1}{4}$ cups
1 lb flour	4 cups	$\frac{3}{4}$ pint	2 cups
1 lb granulated or castor sugar	2 cups	1 pint	$2\frac{1}{2}$ cups
		$1\frac{1}{2}$ pints	$3\frac{3}{4}$ cups
1 lb icing sugar	3 cups	2 pints	5 cups ($2\frac{1}{2}$ pints)
8 oz rice	1 cup		

Note: When making any of the recipes in this book, only follow one set of measures as they are not interchangeable.

Kitchen Sense

When working against time, it's essential that a kitchen is well planned and organised and that the store cupboard is well stocked. Short-cut cookery does not necessarily demand a huge supply of convenience foods; on the contrary, a clever cook will use them to supplement fresh foods. It does, however, require accurate seasoning, careful use of herbs and spices and attractive presentation in the way of garnishes and decoration.

Every cook should go through her kitchen with care, checking that not only does she have a good selection of equipment, but that the pieces she is most likely to use frequently are placed in the most convenient drawers, cupboards or corners of the kitchen. It's far better to put away altogether casseroles or saucepans that are never used, and to keep cutlery drawers filled only with knives and gadgets in daily use. Make sure you have one drawer filled with ready-cut paper liners for tins, kitchen foil, greaseproof paper, polythene bags for storing foods and a roll of cling film wrap — ideal for covering foods in the refrigerator.

Always prepare a list before you go shopping and stick to it. Meals planned ahead save time and are always more economical — shopping bought in a haphazard manner can be very expensive. Since canned foods keep indefinitely, try over a period of time to build up a sensible and good stock. If the housekeeping allows one week, buy in a few extra cans of food, as they may come in handy another week when the budget is tight or time is short. There are many new and interesting products on the market nowadays. Don't be afraid to try something a little unusual. Read all labels carefully before buying to avoid making mistakes.

Kitchen notebooks are great time savers. Keep two, one with tear-out pages to jot down ingredients low in the store cupboard — this way you'll never forget to order foods and won't get caught out for want of an important ingredient, just when you need it most. Attach a pencil with string to the book so members of the family don't keep running off with it! Keep the second book as a recipe collection, and note down ideas of your own or recipes from friends. Take an interest in cooking and swap recipes with other girl friends and stick in ideas you like from magazines.

Spoon measures for speed

Many cooks claim that they never measure ingredients at all, but this is a haphazard way of working and any cook who wants to ensure reasonably good results when she is cooking, must measure the ingredients in some way — certainly in all fairness to the recipe she is following. Not all cooks are fortunate enough to have proper weighing scales but spoon measures can be quite accurate enough. Don't use spoon measures for large quantities of liquid. When you are following recipes, however, watch for descriptions of consistency, positions in the oven, cooking times and check that your recipe is following instructions given. It may help to invest in a set of measuring spoons, which are graded from 1·25 ml/$\frac{1}{4}$ teaspoon to 15 ml/1 tablespoon.

A cook's tools

The best short cuts in all kitchen work come from having the right equipment to work with. Tools may be as simple and necessary as a set of knives, or as specialised as a larding needle or a raised pie mould. Anyone who cooks without the equipment she needs is not only short-handed but much slower.

Knives A minimum number of knives in a kitchen should be one medium-sized knife for chopping, a smaller one for preparing vegetables, a saw-edged knife for breads, and a sharp, fine knife for carving.

To chop parsley or vegetables finely, always use the heel of the knife. First, using the whole blade, cut the vegetables up coarsely, then chop finely holding the tip of the blade with the left fore-finger and the thumb and with the right hand work the blade up and down very quickly, moving back and forwards over the ingredients. To slice vegetables, keep the tip of the blade on the board, raise and lower the knife handle, slicing as you feed the vegetables under the blade.

Remember, too, that a good sharp kitchen knife will cut delicate cakes far better than a blunt cake knife or a saw-edged knife, especially if the cake is covered or filled with frosting. For a special cake that needs to be cut into neat, attractive slices — perhaps some fabulous dessert or a child's birthday cake — take a confectioner's tip. A warm knife blade softens its way quickly through a frosting or cream and doesn't drag, spoiling the appearance. The easiest way to do this is to fill a jug with hot water, dip the knife blade in to heat for a

moment, shake away the drips and then cut the slice quickly. Clean and dip the knife between each cut — sounds like a lot of work but it pays appearance-wise.

Wooden spoons Wooden spoons are best for cooking — they don't scrape or mark the base of a pan and they stand up to high temperatures without getting too hot to hold. There are many different shapes made to get round the edges of pans but the best is the old-fashioned oval spoon. The correct way to stir the contents in a saucepan is to stir once round the sides of the pan then across the middle using a zig-zag movement from side to side, then back round the sides again. Stir continuously like this and you cover the base to prevent burning and keep the contents moving.

Use wooden spoons for creaming or beating mixtures but never for folding in ingredients. The blunt edge of a wooden spoon tends to knock out air in a light mixture; the cutting edge of a metal spoon is more satisfactory to use. One rubber spatula is handy in a kitchen for cleaning out mixing basins. Treat yourself to at least half a dozen spoons of different sizes — I keep mine, handles down in a stone jar near the cooker.

Basins and bowls Never skimp on the number of basins and bowls; keep a good selection both large and small. Large bowls are handy for heavy fruit cakes or whipped up mixtures with a good deal of volume, and small basins can be used for moulding jellies and desserts or for steaming puddings. To save time when following recipes, measure the volume of your pudding basins with water, then mark it in red nail varnish on the base of each bowl — this way you can quickly see whether it's a 900-ml, 1·15- or 1·4-litre/$1\frac{1}{2}$-, 2- or $2\frac{1}{2}$-pint pudding basin, whichever the recipe calls for. This same idea could apply to pie dishes and cake tins.

When creaming butter and sugar or when beating eggs and sugar mixtures — cut working time in half by warming the basin first with hot water. Stand the base of the bowl on a damp sponge square and it won't move while you are working. Hold the basin low — somewhere at hip level — it's less tiring to mix.

Pastry and chopping boards Always keep two boards, a large one for pastry and a smaller one for chopping — both should be at least 2·5-cm/1-inch thick. Wood, being a poor conductor of heat, provides a cool, non-slippery surface for working pastry. Best for yeast doughs, too, since the warmed mixture doesn't lose too

much temperature from being worked on a very cold surface. When using the chopping board, crush garlic in a corner and use the same one every time. Even after washing, the garlic can flavour other foods prepared on the same board.

Rolling pin The rolling pin used by a professional cook is just a simple straight piece of wood. This is because even pressure on the pin is essential when rolling out pastry or dough for even rising. The palms of the hands should be placed on the pin, roll towards and away from you with quick sharp strokes. The tendency when rolling, if using handles on a pin, is to put too much pressure on the outside edges and not enough in the middle. When rolling out dough, sprinkle flour from a dredger — another valuable piece of kitchen equipment. This way you avoid sprinkling too much flour over the working surface — remember, too, it's best to flour the pin, never the pastry.

A rolling pin is useful for beating out meat thinly — wet the rolling pin and working surface with cold water, then meat won't stick to either.

Hand whisks Different ones are designed, each for a special purpose. A balloon whisk, so named for its shape, is right for beating up egg whites or mixtures which need aerating. The slim plain whisks or the curly-edged variety are marvellous for beating sauces to a smooth consistency. Flat whisks are better for beating batter or pancake mixtures although I prefer to beat them with a wooden spoon. Remember that small quantities of ingredients can be whisked together with a fork, and single egg whites come up faster if beaten on a flat plate with a knife.

Kitchen scissors A good pair of kitchen scissors is indispensable — besides using them for the obvious such as snipping, cutting and trimming, let them do difficult chopping tasks as well. Washed herbs or parsley in a teacup can be snipped up finely. Scissors are ideal for cutting glacé fruits, dates or marshmallows — dip scissors in hot water before each snipping and they won't stick together.

Cooling tray At least two cooling trays are necessary — cakes cool without sweating and pastries or biscuits become crisp when cooled on a wire tray where air circulates around. Newly baked cakes and biscuits are very fragile, so handle carefully — cakes should cool for at least five minutes in the tin before turning out.

Cooling trays make excellent racks for icing cakes or coating cold, cooked meats with aspic jelly. Place a flat plate underneath, to catch the drips. Spoon over the icing or jelly; any excess mixture which runs into the plate underneath can be returned to the basin and re-used. Leave on the tray until coating has set firm.

Forcing bags and tubes These bags can be used for piping whipped cream, meringue, choux pastry and mashed potato, which make even a simple recipe look more professional. When using the bag, always have the seam on the outside and place in the required nozzle before filling. Fold back a cuff at the top and then spoon in the mixture until three-quarters full, then turn back the cuff and close the bag. One word of warning — never try to pipe a lumpy mixture; this particularly applies to mashed potato. An extra few minutes beating saves hours of despair.

Flan rings or quiche tins A flan ring has no base and should be set on a flat baking tray before use — a quiche tin usually has a loose base so that the baked mixture can be lifted from the tin. Both are designed for baking pastry cases either with a filling in or for filling afterwards. Once lined with the pastry, to bake the case blind, that is, with no filling, the centre of the unbaked flan must be weighted down in order to keep a flat base. For this, special baking beans, either dried haricot beans, macaroni or rice, may be used if placed on a circle of paper, otherwise crumpled kitchen foil is most suitable. When baking time is almost completed the contents in the centre of the flan and the ring should be gently lifted away and the pastry case returned to the oven to become nice and crisp. The baking beans used should be allowed to cool and then stored in a jar where they are kept only for this purpose.

Best sizes of flan rings to have in a kitchen are 15-cm/6-inch flan rings for pies or tarts serving four portions, and a 20-cm/8-inch ring for larger recipes serving six to eight portions.

Baking tins and trays Any cook's collection of cake and baking tins depends on her interest in baking. Deep round cake tins are best for fruit cakes and the average recipe goes into a 20-cm/8-inch round tin; a 25-cm/10-inch tin is suitable for Christmas or special occasion cakes. Always have a pair of shallow sponge cake tins, 15-18cm/6-7 inches being the average recipe size; if possible a pair of 20-cm/8-inch tins as

well. Always have two of any size as sponge cakes are most often baked in pairs. For quick reference, mark the sizes in red nail varnish on the sides of the tins. Keep a small and a large loaf tin for quick breads; a 20- or 23-cm/8- or 9-inch tube or ring tin; a shallow baking or Swiss roll tin and possibly a large and a small roasting tin — always useful for baking gingerbreads, or honey cake, besides roasting. Keep at least two, if not more baking trays — useful for cookies, pies, flans and scones.

When lining cake tins, it's such a waste to cut round paper liners from sheets of greaseproof paper. Use squares of paper for round tins — cut several at a time and keep in a kitchen drawer. Remember as long as two thirds of the base of a round tin is covered the cake will lift out easily. For a square tin or Swiss roll tin, cut a strip of paper the width of the base and long enough to run up opposite sides of the tin. Loosen unlined sides with a knife before turning out.

Pots and pans It is best to buy a set of three or four different-sized, good quality saucepans with lids. A wise cook invests in one small, heavy-based saucepan of excellent quality for making sauces. Heavy, good quality pans may be tiresome to lift but they cook more evenly and burn far less frequently than thin cheap pans. A cast-iron frying pan is unbeatable for even frying; often two frying pans will cut down on cooking time. Besides the obvious a frying pan may be used to make a plain or soufflé omelette. Non-stick, silicone-lined pans are super for scrambled egg mixtures which normally stick and take hours of cleaning afterwards. Always wash frying pans after use — store small omelette pans in polythene bags to protect them from the damp atmosphere and dust, and rub a little olive oil into the surface of a cast-iron one. To season a new iron pan, heat about 1 tablespoon oil and plenty of kitchen salt together. Continue to heat until the salt begins to brown — then clean the inside of the pan with absorbent paper.

Casseroles Pretty oven-to-table casserole dishes speed up serving time considerably. The most useful ones are the heavy glazed, cast-iron type. These may be set over direct heat and can be used for frying, thus cutting out frying pans or saucepans necessary for initial frying for stews or casseroles — this being done directly in the casserole. Always have one medium-sized and one very large casserole — remember that

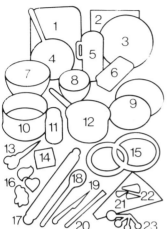

1 Bun tins
2 Baking tray
3 Cooling rack
4 Omelette pan
5 Blender
6 Loaf tin
7 Mixing bowl
8 Pudding basin
9 Quiche tins
10 Nylon sieve
11 Flour dredger
12 Saucepan
13 Kitchen scissors
14 Food timer
15 Fluted flan rings
16 Cutters
17 Rolling pin
18 Wooden spoon
19 Cook's knife
20 Pastry brush
21 Forcing bag
22 Piping tubes
23 Set of measuring spoons

even for only four servings, recipes calling for four chicken joints, oxtail or other bulky ingredients need space.

Always lightly grease the inside of a casserole with a buttered paper before using – it's much easier to clean out afterwards. If you're serving a meal cooked in the oven-to-table ware, clean away any gravy or cooking stains by rubbing with the damp corner of a teacloth using table salt as an abrasive.

Sieves For most recipes an ordinary wire sieve serves the purpose whether to sift dry ingredients, purée soups or strain sauces. The old-fashioned hair sieves on a wooden frame are now usually made in nylon with a plastic handle. It's a wise idea to have one of each in a kitchen. When working, it's a good idea to keep one sieve always dry and use only for sifting dry mixtures and to use the other for straining liquid ingredients. Nylon sieves are essential for sieving icing sugar or acid fruit or vegetable mixtures, or for any recipe where the food might be discoloured or tainted by the wire.

Cutters Cutters are not an essential part of kitchen equipment but, like so many smaller implements, add the finishing touches that are important in cookery. Sharp metal cutters are the best – it's a good idea to buy a set with a tin for storing them. When cutting out scones or biscuits, spoon a little flour to one side of your working surface and dip the cutter first in the flour each time before cutting the dough. This helps prevent the dough – especially a soft scone dough – from sticking to the cutter. With a plain cutter, press down and twist sharply to one side to make sure the dough is cut, then lift away. With fluted or shaped cutters, press down sharply and firmly but do not twist, otherwise the decorative edge is spoilt.

Food timer Burning or over-cooking wastes time and energy and causes disappointment, too. A timer keeps you up to the minute – and if you're working or sitting in another part of the house, carry it with you, if you're inclined to be forgetful.

Pressure cooker, food mixer or blender All three undoubtedly save time, in particular the pressure cooker and blender. A food mixer allows you to get on with other jobs while it works, but as with all equipment, work out carefully where it does actually save time and cut down on long tedious jobs before using it. Lengthy cooking of meat, casseroles, soups or puddings make a

pressure cooker invaluable. To blend or purée soups, fruit or fruit drinks takes only a jiffy in the blender, and the tiring whisking of eggs and sugar mixtures, or whipping up gelatine mixtures, can be done with ease on the mixer.

Setting up a store

A clever cook always has a well-stocked store cupboard. Then she's never in a fix for a quick meal or caught out when unexpected guests call. Choose items for the store cupboard carefully and don't buy on the spur of the moment. Once you've mastered a few recipes that can be quickly prepared, see that you always have the necessary ingredients for them in stock. On the other hand, be generous with your collection of dried herbs and seasonings. Keep in plenty of bottled sauces, ketchups and chutneys. Besides the basic foods in a store cupboard, never be without such ingredients as mustard, stock cubes, concentrated tomato purée, oil or vinegar. In glass jars keep plenty of walnuts, flaked almonds, glacé cherries and angelica — many quick desserts depend on a pretty decoration. Savoury recipes depend on an effective garnish — always try to have fresh tomatoes, lemons and onions. Keep parsley in the refrigerator. Town cooks may find it difficult always to have fresh parsley on hand, but try a greengrocer's tip. Buy the nicest bunch of tightly-curled, green parsley you can find. Wash in cold water, shake off all the moisture and place in a polythene bag. Exclude the air and fasten the neck of the bag with a twist tie — this keeps the parsley fresher longer.

Learn which brands of canned foods you prefer — experiment with different kinds and don't buy, a second time, the ones you dislike. Remember always to wipe the tops of canned foods with a damp cloth before opening — this prevents harmful dust from storage contaminating the contents.

Soups Always keep a few cans of cream and condensed or packet soups on hand — they can provide a substantial first course. In summer, tomato soup, vichyssoise or some of the more exotic kinds can be served chilled.

Fish Stock up with two or three cans of sardines in olive oil — they are useful for hors d'oeuvre or salads. Canned tuna fish or salmon are also useful tossed in cold dressings for salads, or for tossing in a well-

Assorted breads and rolls made with bread mixes (see page 21)

19

seasoned, hot parsley or cheese sauce, and they can be served on hot toast with salad as an accompaniment. Cans of shrimps, prawns or anchovies can be used in open sandwiches, for cocktail snacks, as an hors d'oeuvre, in a sauce, over fish or as a filling for vol-au-vent cases. Soft herring roes and pilchards in tomato sauce are useful for snack meals.

Cooked ham, luncheon meat and corned beef These are good buys. They make excellent cold suppers served with boiled new potatoes, tossed in butter and chives, or with cold potato mayonnaise and tossed green salad. Always serve with mustard, pickles or chutneys. Slices of pork luncheon meat can be egg-and-breadcrumbed and fried in butter, and sliced ham could be served in a hot parsley or mustard sauce.

Stewed steak, minced beef and frankfurter sausages They can be quickly heated and, with additions such as fried mushrooms, canned tomatoes, whole carrots or small whole cooked onions, can make the fillings for pies or the basis for casseroles.

Vegetables Always have canned tomatoes in stock — 425-g/15-oz size is the most useful — and small (64-g/2¼-oz size) cans of tomato purée. Both are invaluable for adding flavour to casseroles and many sauces, as are cans of small whole carrots, butter beans, mushrooms or whole new potatoes. Use celery hearts for snack meals, and whole kernel sweet corn, drained and heated with butter and salt, for a quick vegetable.

Spanish rice, savoury risotto and canned ravioli Topped with plenty of extra grated cheese and browned under the grill these are delicious served with a tossed salad and hot bread. Add sautéed mushrooms or flaked fish to Spanish rice for extra portions. Canned risotto heated through can be served with grilled sausages or hamburgers.

Cook-in-sauces Cook-in-sauces are useful to have on hand and can be used to produce a casserole or tasty chicken dish with a minimum of effort. To use these, you must appreciate that they are not 'pour over' sauces, nor are they created to be tasted direct from the can. Best results are achieved by cooking meat, fish or poultry in the sauce of your choice. The sauce penetrates the food and enhances the flavour, and the consistency of the sauce does not deteriorate with lengthy cooking times.

Canned fruit, instant whips and puddings These help to make trifles and dessert creams in no time at all and they can be topped with glacé cherries, grated nuts or chocolate. Stock up with fruit jellies and evaporated milk for making a quick mousse; creamed rice and a variety of canned fruits are always useful. Canned apple purée is invaluable to serve as a sauce or dessert, and white peaches are particularly delicious if heated in the oven in their own syrup, with a tablespoon of sherry or brandy.

Keep one or two ready-made pie fillings in stock. One can is usually too small for deep dish pies but excellent for quick plate pies — buy ready-made pastry.

Macaroni, spaghetti and long-grain rice Always keep plenty since they form the basis for so many meals. Keep a good supply of cheese to accompany pasta dishes. A jar of grated Parmesan cheese stored in the refrigerator comes in handy.

Bread mixes Using a bread mix for home baked bread and rolls is definitely a saving of time. *White bread* and *brown bread* mixes are available. The 840-g/1 lb 14-oz bags provide sufficient mix to make three medium-sized loaves. The 283-g/10-oz sachets make one medium-sized loaf. The dried yeast in these mixes is very finely powdered and distributed throughout the flour rather in the same way as the raising agent is mixed through self-raising flour. The resulting dough requires kneading for only five minutes and just one proving is necessary to get a good-textured loaf.

You can make a brown cob loaf, a white cottage or a plaited loaf and, of course, you can make rolls from either mix. For added flavour and crunchiness sprinkle loaves or rolls with sesame seeds or cracked wheat before baking. With a little imagination you can adapt the bread dough for use as a pizza base to go along with your favourite savoury topping mix. Store a bread mix in a cool dry place just as you would flour, preferably in the bag with the top folded or twisted down and remember that it has a shelf life of two weeks once opened. If you have a freezer it could be a sensible use of time and oven heat to batch-bake rolls for packed meals or bread for tea. *(Illustrated on page 18)*

Food storage in the refrigerator
A refrigerator is an invaluable asset to any kitchen — besides keeping food clean and fresh, it allows the

cook to re-organise her shopping since perishable foods may now be kept longer. Shopping done at off-peak periods is always quickest and easiest, and a busy cook will find her shopping time cut in half if she plans with this in mind.

Obviously, fresh perishable foods cannot be stored indefinitely, the exact time limit depending on how fresh they are when purchased. To save time before shopping, ideas and a list must be carefully worked out. It sounds dull, but if the menus can be roughly planned for each day, not only can you get in all food required and save last minute shopping, but you can also plan the work so that you can prepare as much as possible beforehand, when you have the time.

Casseroles can be made in advance, or sauces prepared ahead and covered. If you plan on using pastry several times, make it all at once and leave the surplus in a polythene bag in the refrigerator. Actually it makes better pastry than freshly made dough, because it's rested and cool. Prepared fruit desserts or a creamy gâteau can be prepared a day ahead for dinner parties and will keep perfectly.

All food stored in the refrigerator must be protected properly since the action of refrigeration actually draws moisture. Flavours of different foods in the refrigerator will not be absorbed by each other if they are stored in containers or kept wrapped or covered. For this reason, always have rolls of kitchen foil, waxed paper (grease-proof paper is no use because it is absorbent and allows evaporation to take place) and cling film wrapping. The latter is very handy for placing over cut surfaces of cakes, cheese or fresh fruit as the fine surface of the paper clings to the surface on which it is placed. Plenty of plastic containers with airtight lids, and polythene bags are useful, too.

Milk and cream Wipe bottles clean and put in the space provided. Milk will keep perfectly fresh for two or three days. Nice for chilled milk drinks and iced coffee. Dairy cream will keep for three or four days; if the top on the bottle or carton is broken, cover with an extra piece of foil — cream will absorb other flavours quickly. Soured cream, which is very useful for making sauces for cold meats and salads in summer, will keep up to a week; so will yogurt — fruit-flavoured ones are useful to keep in the refrigerator for desserts.

Always store one or two small cans of evaporated milk in the refrigerator – place a small can in a saucepan and cover with cold water. Bring slowly to the boil and simmer for 15 minutes. Then cool and chill. in the refrigerator. It whips up beautifully if treated this way and keeps for months.

Butter and cooking fats Leave in original wrapping – these give sufficient protection. Butter and cooking fats keep for two to three weeks. Suet or clarified dripping will keep almost indefinitely near the base of the cabinet. Soft margarine remains at spreading consistency and it's a good idea to keep a carton in the refrigerator for all-in-one cakes (see page 114). In general, remove butter to be used in baking sometime before use to allow it to soften for quicker mixing.

Eggs Do not wash eggs but store in the compartment provided. Store no longer than two weeks. Before using in cooking, remove from the refrigerator and allow to warm up to room temperature. A better volume comes from egg whites if they are not chilled in the refrigerator. Egg whites at room temperature will absorb more air. Beat them in a cool corner of the kitchen, however, even on the back doorstep – the cooler the air incorporated the more the mixture rises in the oven.

Egg whites or egg yolks left over from cooking may be kept for one or two days. Collect whites in a covered container or jar, and keep yolks in a small cup or basin covered with water. Add yolks to sauces, custards or scrambled egg. Mark number of egg whites on outside of jar or container. If you forget, it doesn't matter – simply tip them out slowly from the jar. The albumen of egg white tends to cling to itself and you can count them as they fall.

Fish Fish should be eaten as soon as possible; never keep fresh fish or shellfish for longer than 24 hours. Wipe or rinse under cold water and store unwrapped but covered with a sheet of waxed or cellophane paper. Fresh salmon or salmon trout will keep for two days. Cooked fish or shellfish will keep one or two days.

Fresh meat and poultry Always remove meat and poultry from the butcher's wrapping, unless it has been purchased from a supermarket where it is sealed in a vacuum pack. Raw meat should be lightly covered with waxed paper or foil and put in the coldest part near the refrigerator unit or in the special meat tray. Bacteria in

meat attack moist cut surfaces; for this reason a large joint or whole unstuffed chicken will keep in perfect condition for two or three days and small cuts a slightly shorter time — two days. On the other hand minced meat, which has many cut surfaces, and offal should be stored for no longer than 24 hours.

Bacon Smoked or cured joints can be stored in the original wrapping if vacuum sealed, otherwise they should be wrapped in waxed paper or foil and placed on a low shelf. Bacon rashers will keep for one week.

Pastry Prepared puff, rough puff or flaky pastry wrapped in waxed paper or foil will keep for one to two days. Prepared shortcrust pastry will keep too, but it is better to keep a rubbed-in shortcrust pastry mixture to which water need only be added to make a pastry dough. A basic rubbed-in pastry mixture will keep for two to three weeks in a covered jar or polythene bag (see page 118).

Cheeses Hard cheeses keep perfectly for two or three weeks or more in a polythene bag, wrapped in aluminium foil or in a refrigerator box. Cheese spreads and cream cheese wrapped in foil keep up to a week, and cottage cheese keeps for three to five days; very soft perishable cheeses keep for 24 hours.

Whenever serving cheese simply on its own, remove it from the refrigerator at least an hour before serving, so it may come up to room temperature for the best flavour. Pieces of left-over cheese can be used to make potted cheese or spreads. Grate small pieces of left-over Cheddar cheese, allow to dry and then store in a screw-topped jar. Keep up to a week.

Home-made potted meats, pâtés and spreads Keeping time may depend a little on the recipe, but on the whole any cooked potted meat or pâté will keep up to one week and it should be stored either in the container in which it was cooked, or in a special covered pot. Cheese or meat spread will keep covered for up to a week.

Casseroles cooked in advance and left-over cooked food Prepare any favourite casserole recipe, cool quickly and store in the refrigerator covered with a lid. Casseroles can be made one day in advance but no longer. Omit stirring in any last minute ingredients such as egg yolks or cream. When required, reheat in a moderate oven (180°C, 350°F, Gas Mark 4) for 30 minutes, or until bubbling hot.

Sliced, cooked left-over meat should be covered with cling film wrapping and cooked soups poured into a basin and covered with a plate; both keep one or two days. Always remove cooked stuffing from chicken or turkey carcass and store separately.

Vegetables and fruit Salad vegetables and citrus fruit benefit most from being stored in the refrigerator and keep three to five days. Vitamin C deteriorates rapidly at room temperature and when exposed to light. In this case, green vegetables such as spinach, cabbage and broccoli are better if washed, prepared and stored in a polythene bag in the refrigerator. All salad vegetables should be washed and placed in the vegetable crisper.

Swing washed lettuce dry in a tea towel to remove moisture and store in a polythene bag in the refrigerator, where it will crisp up nicely. Never toss salad in any dressing until ready to serve; the acid in the vinegar makes lettuce go limp.

Cut lemons or other citrus fruit should be placed in a polythene bag, low down in the refrigerator; keep up to one week. Store soft summer fruits for one to two days only.

Some fruits, such as melon, need only be chilled for an hour or so before serving. When cut, keep the slices closely covered to prevent the aroma from flavouring other foods. Bananas, however, dislike the cold and will quickly go black if stored in the refrigerator. Open canned or left-over cooked vegetables will keep up to three days — best to remove from the can.

Salad dressings and sauces During summer months it's a good idea to make up a large quantity of oil and vinegar dressing and store in the refrigerator in a screw-topped jar. Follow your favourite recipe and make 300 ml/$\frac{1}{2}$ pint at a time; it will keep up to two or three weeks — remember to shake well before using. Home-made mayonnaise will keep in covered plastic containers for one to two weeks. Any fresh cream or soured cream dressing will keep up to three days.

Mineral water, fruit juices, syrups and wine It's inadvisable to take up valuable space storing these in the refrigerator. If, however, you plan on using them, tonic water and bitter lemon can be chilled and cans of tomato juice, fruit juices, beer, cider or lager can be kept chilled. White wine to be served with a meal is nicest chilled for an hour or so beforehand.

Home-made fruit syrups for quick milk shakes are handy for children — they will keep for two or three weeks.

Ice cubes Keep ice trays always filled; individual plastic ice-cube moulds are handy for single ice cubes. For a large supply, keep extra cubes in a polythene bag in the frozen foods section. Either make cubes in trays from which the cubes can be removed by dipping in cold water, or place the cubes on a tray and open freeze for five to ten minutes just to dry the outside surfaces. Then tip into a large bag for storage and they will not stick together. To make decorative ice cubes for summer drinks, add maraschino cherries, pieces of lemon or orange peel or food colouring to the ice tray before adding the water.

Shortcrust pastry, scone or cake ready-mixes It really depends on how often you plan on using these mixes as to whether it's worth making them or not. Small quantities of left-over stews or casseroles can be made into pies with extra meat from a can; ready-made pie fillings or bottled or canned fruits can fill fruit pies or flans, made with shortcrust pastry. With extra sugar added, the mix can make a crumble topping for fresh or bottled fruit.

Storing food in a freezer
Much of what has been said about storing food in a refrigerator applies to freezers as well, but of course there is a multitude of other time and money saving possibilities if you own a freezer.

It's useful to know that a freezer is more economical to run if it is kept well stocked. To make the most of a freezer, take advantage of a glut of any fruit or vegetable, and put away a good store of them for any time when they are expensive or not available in the shops. While talking about vegetables, it is a good time saving ruse to pack up individual bags of mixed casserole vegetables cut ready for use. Of course the preparation takes time, but if you have a few hours to spare, it will save time later when you are rushed.

It is not necessary to prepare dozens of complete meals, better to make sure you have a few standby basics such as beefburgers, baked pastry cases, prepared fish cakes, home-made soups and uncooked pastry — all great time savers. The main objects of a freezer are to help store foods in a state in which they are quick to use, to enable the busy housewife to buy in bulk at a

smaller cost, and to preserve garden produce when it is in season and when there is time.

If you get a chance to bake on a large scale, it is worth preparing an extra quantity to put in the freezer, in this way you can save on cooking costs by baking only once, and also save on time, as it takes very little extra time to mix up a double quantity.

There are some foods which lend themselves admirably to freezing, but some such as single cream, eggs in their shells, watery vegetables, particularly lettuce, avocados and fruits such as bananas are not recommended for freezing. Eggs are fine if incorporated into cakes or other floury mixtures, but in a raw or hard-boiled form they are impossible to freeze. Fish, if you are lucky enough to have a fisherman in the house, are a useful standby for a meal and are easy to freeze once cleaned and gutted and thaw quite fast when you need them.

Many people keep enough chicken joints in the freezer to deal with at least one meal — being small they don't take long to thaw.

Where meat is concerned, most butchers have offers for freezer owners, and if you can get together with friends and share a whole animal for the freezer, you not only save money, but you also have a good selection of cuts to choose from when planning a meal.

If you do want to prepare a meal in advance and store it in the freezer, it is worth remembering that sauces made with ordinary household flour turn watery on thawing, so it is best to use cornflour as the thickening agent.

Apart from freezing fresh vegetables yourself, there are also a number of stores now which sell frozen foods in bulk bags, which are considerably cheaper than the small packs sold in most supermarkets, and are splendid for emergency meals.

Frozen foods
Unless for immediate consumption within 24 hours, frozen foods should be stored in the frozen food compartment of a refrigerator. Accurate storage of frozen foods depends on the temperature of the compartment — in other words, the lower the temperature the longer the food will keep. There is now a new method of guidance for the home cook which consists of star marking on both frozen foods and the frozen compartment.

If your refrigerator has one star, it means the frozen food compartment operates at under −6°C, 21°F and will keep frozen foods for one week. With two stars, the frozen food compartment operates below −12°C, 10°F and the frozen foods will keep for a month. Three stars and a temperature not higher than −18°C, 0°F means that the foods will keep for three months.

A good frozen food compartment in your refrigerator gives plenty of scope for stocking up with quick frozen foods. Select the ones you buy carefully and plan on using them.

Vegetables All vegetables can be cooked while still frozen, and to preserve the food values, cook them in the very minimum amount of boiling salted water for the length of time stated on the packet.

Fish Most fish fillets are individually wrapped and need not be thawed before cooking. Plaice fillets should be separated from their polythene wrapping; cod and haddock steaks removed from their polythene envelopes. Follow the cooking instructions given on the backs of the cartons for frying or grilling. Otherwise allow to thaw and then use in any recipe.

Fish fingers and fish portions come already coated with breadcrumbs; they need not be thawed, and are best fried or grilled and served with tomato or tartare sauce.

Kippers and smoked haddock in polythene are best immersed in the bag in boiling water for a few minutes.

Meat Meat dishes such as steaklets, beefburgers and cheeseburgers may be grilled or fried immediately after opening the packet, without being thawed. Cook-in-the-bag meat dishes, including casseroles and curries and sliced beef in gravy in foil trays, may also be cooked without thawing.

Poultry on the other hand must be allowed to thaw to ensure complete cooking. Buy the bird the day before you want to cook it. For a chicken casserole or special recipe for grilling or frying, buy individually packed quartered chickens or chicken joints.

Dessert items and fruit Cream cakes, éclairs, mousses and frozen fruit all need to be thawed before serving. Simply remove from their carton or bag and leave them on a plate or in a dish at room temperature for an hour or two.

Grilling and frying

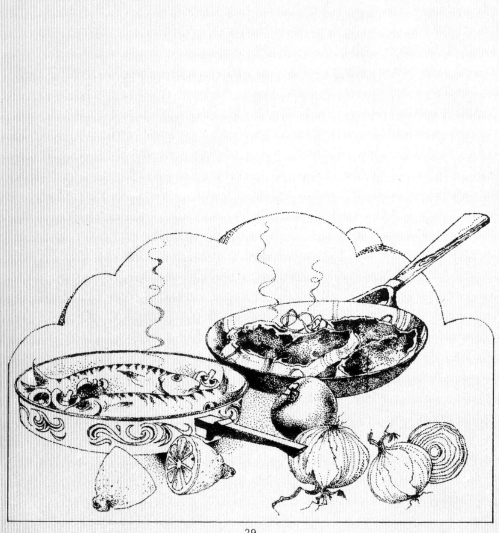

Both grilling and frying are simple and quick methods of cooking. Both depend on food that cooks quickly and evenly, which therefore has to be of good quality. There are lots of ways to make grilled or fried foods more interesting — food may be marinated beforehand, spicy bastes may be used while grilling, or cooked foods may be served with flavoured butters.

In the case of both methods of cooking, high heat should be used initially, then a more gentle heat used to cook the food through. Garnishes are important for food cooked in such a simple manner — sprigs of parsley, chopped parsley, lemon butterflies or wedges are but a few suggestions — see page 122 for others.

MEAT TO CHOOSE FOR GRILLING

Steak Only the best cuts of meat are suitable for grilling — cheaper cuts tend to become dry and tough when cooked by this quick method.

Choose from the following steaks: *fillet* which should always be cut in fairly thick slices by the butcher; *rump* which is best bought in one large piece and then cut into portions after grilling; *porterhouse* which is cut individually — many cooks say this is more reliable as far as tenderness goes than any other steak; *frying steak* which means anything — whether good quality or not depends on the price; *minute* or *quick-fry steak* which is cut very thinly and then beaten flat so that it cooks quickly.

Trim away any excess fat from around the meat, season both sides with salt and freshly ground pepper and brush all over with oil or melted butter. Steak should be cooked under a high heat to seal in the juices — then reduce the heat and cook at a lower temperature according to the thickness of the meat, first on one side and then the other. Take care not to prick the meat while turning. When the meat is ready a good cook can tell by the 'feel' of the meat. Press the centre of the meat with a forefinger; if the flesh gives easily under the pressure, the meat is rare — very red with the centre still raw. If flesh resists but is still a little soft, it is medium rare — red in the centre and cooked round the edges. If the meat feels firm, then the steak is cooked right through.

Lamb Choose from the following: *best end of neck cutlets, loin* and *chump chops.* Check there are no splintered pieces of bone especially in the neck cutlets. If serving garnished with a cutlet frill — then trim the fat away neatly at the top of the bone, otherwise it's not necessary. The larger loin chops can be boned; the butcher will do this or prepare them yourself using a sharp knife and cut the bone out of the chop. Curl the chop, wrapping the thinner part round the centre piece of meat. Wrap each boned chop with a thin bacon rasher and secure with a skewer or wooden cocktail stick.

Season with salt and pepper and brush both sides with oil or melted butter and grill. For extra flavour, sprinkle with a pinch of dried thyme, pressing it well in before grilling.

Pork Choose *loin chops* — sometimes the larger ones have a kidney included as well. Trim the fat neatly and, using a small knife, cut slits at 1-cm/$\frac{1}{2}$-inch intervals on the fat down the outer edge on a pork chop — this helps to prevent buckling while grilling.

Season with salt and freshly ground pepper or lemon pepper. Pork chops have a delicious sharp sweet flavour if rubbed over with equal parts castor sugar and dry mustard — about 1 teaspoon of each is sufficient for 4 chops — the sugar makes them brown nicely, too.

Chicken Choose *joints* or *small halved poussin.* It is not necessary to remove the skin from chicken joints before cooking; simply trim away any loose pieces. Ask the butcher to halve the poussin for you.

Season with salt and pepper then brush both sides with melted butter or oil — add crushed rosemary or thyme if liked.

Lamb's and calves' kidneys Lamb's or calves' kidneys are the most suitable ones for grilling; of the two, lamb's kidneys are smaller and more readily available. To prepare the kidneys, remove all the protective fatty tissue from the outside, snip away any core and remove outer skin. Slice into each kidney on the *rounded* side, cutting almost through but not quite. Open out the kidneys and skewer in pairs on kitchen skewers. Unless skewered, the kidneys will curl up too much while cooking. Brush with oil and season with salt and freshly ground pepper.

Bacon and gammon rashers *Back rashers* are the leanest; trim away the rind before grilling but no additional fat is needed. *Gammon rashers* are usually cut about 5-mm/$\frac{1}{4}$-inch thick. Trim away any rind with a sharp pair of scissors and nick the fat at intervals to prevent buckling while cooking. If you like a mild flavour, soak gammon rashers in cold water or milk for about 2 hours;

drain and pat dry before cooking. Arrange rashers for grilling with the fat part of each covering the lean part of the next rasher.

Sausages These need no preparation; simply place close together in the grill pan. Brush with oil, to help even browning; do not season.

Times for grilled meats

	Rare	Medium done	Well done
Steak			
1·5-cm/$\frac{3}{4}$-inch thick	3-5 minutes	9-10 minutes	14-15 minutes
2·5-cm/1-inch thick	6-7 minutes	10 minutes	15 minutes
3·5-cm/1$\frac{1}{2}$-inches thick	10 minutes	12-14 minutes	18-20 minutes
Lamb chops		12 minutes	14 minutes
Pork and veal chops (must be well done)			15 minutes
Chicken joints and poussin			18-25 minutes
Kidneys			6-8 minutes
Bacon		2-3 minutes	4 minutes
Sausages			15 minutes

Fish to choose for grilling

Hake, cod and haddock Buy either cutlets or fillets. Wash and trim cutlets; pat dry and season on both sides with salt and pepper. Soak in marinade, if used, or brush fish all over with melted butter.

Mackerel and herrings Whole or boned fish are available. Wash and pat the fish dry. When grilling whole mackerel or herring, cut deep gashes in through the skin on the sides to allow the heat to penetrate. Brush mackerel, but not herrings, with oil before grilling. Serve with wedges of lemon.

Plaice, sole and dabs Whole fish or fish fillets can be bought. Wash sole and pull away the black skin – easiest to ask fishmonger to do this for you. Pat dry then brush with salad oil or melted butter. Place under a fairly hot grill depending on the thickness of the fish; grill on both sides. Grill fish fillets on one side only. Serve with parsley butter, or wedges of lemon and chopped parsley.

Salmon, turbot and halibut Cutlets should be cut about 2·5 cm/1 inch thick. Trim and season with salt and pepper, brush over with oil or melted butter. Grill under a fairly hot grill, turning after 10 minutes. Serve with wedges of lemon and watercress.

Trout Brush whole trout with salad oil and sprinkle with salt and pepper. Place under a hot grill, turning after 5 minutes.

Kippers and bloaters No preparation needed. Place whole fish under a medium grill; no extra fat or seasoning is necessary.

Times for grilled fish

Hake, cod and haddock
Cutlets 5-7 minutes each side
Fillets 8-10 minutes one side

Mackerel
Whole 5-8 minutes each side

Herrings
Whole 3-4 minutes each side
Boned 6-8 minutes one side

Plaice, sole and dabs
Whole 2-4 minutes each side
Fillets 4-6 minutes one side

Salmon, turbot and halibut
Cutlets 10 minutes each side

Trout
Whole 5-10 minutes each side

Kippers
Whole 5 minutes one side

Bloaters
Whole 3-4 minutes each side

Marinades for fried or grilled foods

Marinades can add extra flavour to foods such as fish, chicken or veal, or they can tenderise meat. They usually consist of oil and vinegar or lemon juice, with additional flavourings. Spoon over chicken joints, steaks, chops or fish, arranged in a shallow china or glass dish 15 minutes to 1 hour before cooking. Leave to soak, turning the food occasionally.

All-purpose marinade Mix 3 tablespoons salad oil, 3 tablespoons vinegar (or dry white wine or lemon juice), a seasoning of salt and freshly ground pepper. Add a little chopped onion or crushed clove of garlic, or parsley stalks if liked for extra flavour. Use for chicken joints, chops or steaks.

Egg marinade Ideal to use in any recipe where the meat or fish is to be coated with breadcrumbs before cooking. Blend together 1 egg, 1 teaspoon chopped parsley, little finely grated lemon rind, 1 teaspoon melted butter or salad oil and seasoning of salt and pepper. Beat lightly together with a fork. Use for veal or pork escalopes, white fish fillets or cutlets.

Lemon marinade for fish Combine together 6 tablespoons salad oil, 3 tablespoons vinegar, 1 teaspoon salt, little freshly ground pepper, strained juice of 1 lemon and $\frac{1}{2}$ small onion finely chopped. Use for white fish cutlets or fillets.

Wine marinade for meat Combine together 150 ml/$\frac{1}{4}$ pint red wine, 1 tablespoon salad oil, 1 onion (peeled and sliced), 1 bay leaf, $\frac{1}{2}$ teaspoon dried thyme, $\frac{1}{2}$ teaspoon salt, and little freshly ground pepper.

If liked, this marinade may be used to make a sauce to serve with steak or lamb chops.

Herb marinade for chicken Combine together 3 tablespoons salad oil, 6 tablespoons dry white wine, 1 crushed clove garlic, 1 small onion (finely chopped), 1 teaspoon salt, little freshly ground pepper and $\frac{1}{4}$ teaspoon dried thyme, tarragon or rosemary. Use for chicken joints.

Bastes for grilled foods

Basting food while grilling gives extra flavour and helps prevent dryness. Liquids can be drippings, seasoned butter, vinegar, oil or special sauces. Brush over chops, chicken joints, hamburgers, fish or sausages while grilling and when turning.

Barbecue baste Blend together 2 tablespoons made mustard, $\frac{1}{2}$ teaspoon each pepper and salt, 1 tablespoon soft brown sugar, 2 tablespoons wine vinegar or lemon juice and 3 tablespoons tomato ketchup. Brush over sausages, hamburgers, chops, steak or chicken joints.

Mustard baste Blend together 1 tablespoon vinegar, 1 tablespoon made mustard and 50 g/ 2 oz brown sugar. Brush over chicken joints, sausages, pork chops and steak.

Butter baste Melt 100 g/4 oz butter and stir in 4 tablespoons bottled meat sauce and 3 tablespoons tomato ketchup. Brush over hamburgers, steak and lamb chops.

Spicy baste Combine together 4 tablespoons tomato ketchup, 1 teaspoon Tabasco sauce, 2 tablespoons orange marmalade, 1 tablespoon finely chopped onion, 1 tablespoon salad oil, squeeze of lemon juice and 1 teaspoon made mustard.

Brush over pork or veal chops, chicken joints or hamburgers.

Kebab baste Combine together 3 tablespoons soy sauce, 3 tablespoons pineapple juice and 3 tablespoons thin honey. If liked, marinate the kebabs in the baste first then use as a baste as they are cooking. This is particularly good if pineapple chunks are used in the kebabs along with the meat.

BUTTERS

Grilled or fried foods, when not served with a gravy or sauce, can be topped with delicious flavoured butters. Prepare the butter several hours ahead, then spoon the blended mixture on to a square of kitchen foil. Shape into a roll — twist the ends like a cracker and chill in the refrigerator until quite firm. Then slice and top each piece of cooked meat just before serving. These recipes make enough for four portions. Any butter not used will store in the refrigerator until next time.

Herb butter Blend 2 teaspoons lemon juice and 1 teaspoon dried mixed herbs with 50 g/2 oz butter. Serve with chicken, lamb or pork chops.

Parsley butter Blend a squeeze of lemon juice and 1 tablespoon finely chopped parsley with 50 g/2 oz butter. Serve with steak or fish.

Onion butter Blend 1 teaspoon Worcestershire sauce, $\frac{1}{4}$ teaspoon dry mustard and freshly ground pepper, with 50 g/2 oz butter, until creamy. Then add 2 tablespoons finely chopped or minced onion and 2 tablespoons finely chopped parsley. Serve with steak, lamb or pork chops.

Blue cheese butter Blend 2-3 tablespoons crumbled blue cheese and $\frac{1}{2}$ teaspoon made mustard with 50 g/2 oz butter. Serve with steak.

Lemon butter Blend the finely grated rind and juice of half a lemon and 1 teaspoon castor sugar with 50 g/2 oz butter. Serve with chicken or fish.

Sharp butter Blend 1 level teaspoon dry mustard, dash of onion or celery salt, $\frac{1}{2}$ teaspoon curry powder and a little freshly ground pepper with 50 g/2 oz butter. Serve with steak.

Mustard butter Cream together 50 g/2 oz butter, $\frac{1}{2}$ teaspoon made English mustard, 1 teaspoon chopped parsley and a squeeze of lemon juice. Serve with steak or pork chops.

Mint butter Cream 50 g/2 oz butter until soft, then gradually beat in 1 teaspoon vinegar. Add 3 teaspoons freshly chopped mint and a seasoning of salt and pepper. Serve with lamb chops or chicken.

CHICKEN WITH ROSEMARY

Serves 4
Cooking time about 20 minutes

METRIC		IMPERIAL
4 chicken joints		4 chicken joints
50 g butter		2 oz butter
$\frac{1}{2}$ lemon		$\frac{1}{2}$ lemon
salt and pepper		salt and pepper
4 sprigs of rosemary		4 sprigs of rosemary
8 rashers of bacon		8 rashers of bacon

Wipe the chicken joints and trim away any loose skin. Melt the butter and draw the pan off the heat. Rub the chicken joints over with the cut surface of half a lemon, brush with melted butter, season with salt and freshly ground pepper and place a sprig of rosemary on each joint. Remove the grid from the grill pan and line the pan with a square of kitchen foil, if liked, to catch the juices. Arrange the chicken joints in the pan, skin side down and place under a preheated moderate grill.

Cook the chicken for 10-12 minutes, then turn skin side up. Baste again and cook for a further 10-12 minutes. Brush with melted butter several times during cooking.

Trim the bacon rashers and arrange in the pan along with the chicken 2-3 minutes before end of cooking time.

Serve the grilled chicken joints with the bacon.

Gammon steaks with pineapple

Serves 4
Cooking time 12-15 minutes

METRIC
4 gammon steaks cut about 5 mm or 1 cm thick
little soft brown sugar
25 g butter
1 (227-g) can pineapple rings

IMPERIAL
4 gammon steaks cut about $\frac{1}{4}$ or $\frac{1}{2}$ inch thick
little soft brown sugar
1 oz butter
1 (8-oz) can pineapple rings

Trim any outer rind from the steaks and snip the fat at 5-mm/$\frac{1}{4}$-inch intervals. Rub the fatty part of the gammon with sugar and place a nut of butter on each steak. Place under a preheated grill and cook for about 7-10 minutes. Turn, rub the fat with sugar, baste with the drippings and grill the second sides for about 5 minutes.

Drain the pineapple rings from the can and place a ring on each rasher. Return under the grill until the pineapple is heated through, then serve.

Variation

Spicy gammon steaks Trim the gammon steaks as above and arrange them in an ovenproof dish. Mix together 2 teaspoons dry mustard, 2 teaspoons cinnamon and 100 g/4 oz soft brown sugar and spoon half of this over the gammon. Squeeze the juice from 2 oranges and make it up to 450 ml/$\frac{3}{4}$ pint with the juice drained from a 454-g/16-oz can of peach halves. Pour this around the gammon, cover with foil and bake in a moderate oven (180°C, 350°F, Gas Mark 4) for 45 minutes.

Peel, quarter, core and slice 450 g/1 lb cooking apples, arrange them over the cooked gammon and spoon over the rest of the spice and sugar. Baste with the juices and return, uncovered, to the oven for 30 minutes. Spoon chutney into the peach halves and heat them in the oven for about 10 minutes. Remove the gammon from the juices and keep hot on a serving plate; use 20 g/$\frac{3}{4}$ oz cornflour blended with a little water to thicken the juices. Spoon this sauce over the gammon and serve it hot with the peach halves. *(Illustrated on back jacket)*

Grilled plaice with shrimp sauce (see page 37)

Grilled plaice with shrimp sauce

Serves 4
Cooking time 5-10 minutes

METRIC
2 whole plaice, filleted
salt and pepper
25 g butter, melted
Shrimp sauce
2 (50-g) cartons potted shrimps
squeeze of lemon juice
1 teaspoon finely chopped parsley
Garnish
twists of lemon
sprigs of parsley

Allow two fish fillets per person. Rinse and pat dry then season with salt and pepper and brush with the butter. Place under a hot grill and cook for 5-6 minutes without turning.

Meanwhile empty the potted shrimps into a small saucepan and set over low heat to melt the butter. Add the lemon juice and stir in the parsley. Heat through gently; serve spooned over the fish.
(*Illustrated on page 35*)

IMPERIAL
2 whole plaice, filleted
salt and pepper
1 oz butter, melted
Shrimp sauce
2 (2-oz) cartons potted shrimps
squeeze of lemon juice
1 teaspoon finely chopped parsley
Garnish
twists of lemon
sprigs of parsley

Kebabs

All sorts of tasty combinations of food can be fixed on skewers and grilled. Brush with oil, melted butter or a spicy butter baste while cooking. It's a good idea to buy about six long sharp skewers for recipes such as these. Cook and serve the food on the kebab skewers, then invite guests to push food off on to their own plates, using the prongs of a fork. Serve a tossed salad or cooked rice (see page 5) with the kebabs.

Devilled kidneys and mushrooms

Serves 4
Cooking time about 10 minutes

METRIC
8 lambs' kidneys
8 button mushrooms
Mustard butter
50 g butter
2 tablespoons dry mustard

Remove all protective fatty tissue from around the kidneys, snip away the core and remove the outer skin. Slice into each kidney on the rounded side, cutting almost through but not quite. Open out the kidneys and skewer in pairs on four skewers, alternating each kidney with a mushroom. Set aside while preparing the mustard butter.

Melt the butter in a saucepan over a low heat, taking care not to brown the butter. Draw the pan off the heat and stir in the mustard. Mix well and then using a pastry brush, spread the butter generously over the kebabs. Place the skewers under a preheated moderately hot grill and cook for 8 minutes, brushing with the baste. Turn, brush again with mustard butter and grill for a further 2-3 minutes.
(*Illustrated opposite*)

IMPERIAL
8 lambs' kidneys
8 button mushrooms
Mustard butter
2 oz butter
2 tablespoons dry mustard

Devilled kidneys and mushrooms (see above)

Liver and bacon kebabs

Serves 4
Cooking time 10-15 minutes

METRIC
·100 g bacon rashers
350 g calves' liver, cut into
two slices
4 tomatoes
butter baste (see page 32)

Cut the rinds from the bacon rashers and cut in half. Trim the liver and cut into cubes; roll the bacon rashers around some of the pieces of liver. Thread on to long skewers along with the halved tomatoes. Set aside while preparing the butter baste. With a pastry brush, generously spread the kebabs with the baste. Arrange the skewers under a moderately hot grill and cook for 10-15 minutes, brushing with the butter baste and turning to cook evenly.

IMPERIAL
4 oz bacon rashers
12 oz calves' liver, cut into
two slices
4 tomatoes
butter baste (see page 32)

Scampi and mushroom kebabs with devil sauce

Serves 4
Cooking time 10 minutes

METRIC
1 (227-g) packet frozen
scampi, thawed
about 16 button mushrooms
50 g butter, melted
Devil sauce
150 ml tomato ketchup
2 dashes of Tabasco sauce
1 tablespoon Worcestershire
sauce
3 tablespoons made mustard
1 lemon, cut into wedges

Separate the scampi and pat dry. Wash and trim the button mushrooms and then thread alternately with the scampi on to four kebab skewers and brush thoroughly with the butter.

Combine together the tomato ketchup, Tabasco sauce, Worcestershire sauce and the mustard and then, using a pastry brush, spread generously over the kebabs. Grill under a moderate heat for 5 minutes each side. Serve immediately with wedges of lemon and devil sauce.

IMPERIAL
1 (8-oz) packet frozen
scampi, thawed
about 16 button mushrooms
2 oz butter, melted
Devil sauce
¼ pint tomato ketchup
2 dashes of Tabasco sauce
1 tablespoon Worcestershire
sauce
3 tablespoons made mustard
1 lemon, cut into wedges

Scallop kebabs

Serves 4
Cooking time 10 minutes

METRIC
4 scallops
freshly ground pepper
8 streaky bacon rashers
1 (226-g) can pineapple
cubes
oil or melted butter

Ask the fishmonger to clean the scallops and remove the shell. Rinse and cut each scallop into quarters, then sprinkle with lemon juice and freshly ground black pepper. Trim the bacon rashers and stretch each one using the blade of a knife, flattening them out along a clean working surface. Cut rashers in half and wrap each half round a piece of scallop.

Thread on four long skewers alter-

IMPERIAL
4 scallops
freshly ground pepper
8 streaky bacon rashers
1 (8-oz) can pineapple
cubes
oil or melted butter

nately with pineapple cubes. Brush skewers with oil or melted butter and place under a preheated hot grill. Grill on both sides, turning for even cooking, about 10 minutes in all. Serve at once with hot buttered toast.

FRyiNq

With this method of cooking, recipes can be a little more elaborate. Food is cooked quickly in the pan and if liked a sauce may be made with the pan juices. A good cook will have at least one, if not two or three frying pans — choose the heaviest pan you can afford, preferably a cast iron one. A French sauté pan — a wide shallow pan with a lid — is a good investment; often food initially fried needs further cooking, and sometimes a lid from a large saucepan may be used, or failing that a second frying pan of the same size upturned over the top will do.

Choice of foods for frying are similar to grilling with the additions of liver, and veal or pork escalopes. The choice of fat for frying varies — where a high heat is required use vegetable cooking fat or oil, where flavour is important use butter. Watch the heat when cooking unless quick frying is recommended; ingredients cook more evenly and do not stick when the heat is moderate.

Most foods need a little extra protection against the high heat of frying — a coating of seasoned flour or lightly mixed egg and bread-crumbs is sufficient and adds to the finished appearance, too. Serve with any of the butters given in the grilling section that would be suitable.

Foods to choose for fryiNq

Steak Season steak on both sides with salt and freshly ground black pepper. Fry in hot butter turning once, time according to taste and thickness of meat. *Time* 5-12 minutes.

Liver Buy liver thinly sliced and remove any skin or tough parts. Soak in milk for 1 hour beforehand. Drain and dip both sides in seasoned flour and fry quickly in butter or vegetable fat, turning to brown on both sides. *Time* 5-8 minutes.

Sausages Separate sausages — do not prick them with a fork as this encourages them to burst. Place in a cold frying pan with 15 g/½ oz vegetable fat, lard or dripping and fry gently, turning to brown evenly. *Time* 10-15 minutes.

Lamb chops Season with salt and pepper and a little rosemary, if liked. Fry lamb chops in vegetable fat or dripping, turning to brown both sides. *Time* 15-20 minutes.

Pork chops Trim chops and rub both sides with a mixture of 1 teaspoon each dry mustard and castor sugar, or season with salt, pepper and crushed thyme and dust with flour. Fry in lard or vegetable fat, turning to brown both sides. Cover and cook slowly, turning occasionally. *Time* 20-30 minutes.

Pork tenderloin and veal escalopes Place thin pork tenderloin slices or veal escalopes between sheets of wetted greaseproof paper — this way the paper won't stick to the meat. Beat flat with a rolling pin. Dip both sides of the meat in seasoned beaten egg and then in fresh white breadcrumbs; fry quickly in butter, turning once. Squeeze fresh lemon juice over the meat before serving. *Time* 5-6 minutes.

Chicken joints Trim joints; it's not necessary to remove the skin. Season with salt and pepper and either dip in seasoned flour, or first in lightly beaten egg and then in breadcrumbs or alternatively in melted butter and crushed cornflake crumbs. Place in the frying pan skin side down and fry gently in butter, turning to cook and brown evenly. *Time* 30-35 minutes.

White fish Cod, plaice or haddock should be trimmed, cut into fillets or cutlets, seasoned with salt and pepper and then dipped in beaten egg and toasted breadcrumbs. Fry gently in butter, turning to brown evenly. *Time* 5-10 minutes.

Whole fish Trim fins and scrape away any fish scales. Herring or mackerel can be fried in butter as they are. Trout are nicest dipped in seasoned flour first. *Time* Herring or trout 6-8 minutes. Mackerel 15-20 minutes.

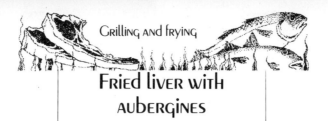

FRIED LIVER WITH AUBERGINES

Serves 4
Cooking time about 20 minutes

METRIC
450 g lambs' liver, cut in thin slices
seasoned flour
oil for frying
2 large aubergines, peeled
squeeze of lemon juice
Garnish
chopped parsley

IMPERIAL
1 lb lambs' liver, cut in thin slices
seasoned flour
oil for frying
2 large aubergines, peeled
squeeze of lemon juice
Garnish
chopped parsley

For the best flavour, liver should be thinly cut and very quickly cooked — over-cooked liver immediately becomes tough, properly cooked liver should still be a little pink in the centre.

Trim the liver, little should be necessary with lambs' liver; on the more coarse livers certain pieces of gristle need snipping away. Dip both sides in seasoned flour. Heat sufficient oil to cover the base of the frying pan. Add the sliced aubergines and fry gently, turning to brown both sides. Add more oil if neccessary to fry all the aubergines. Lift from the pan and keep hot. Add the liver slices and fry quickly for about 2 minutes either side.

Squeeze the lemon juice over the cooked liver and sprinkle with chopped parsley. Lift from the pan and serve with the aubergine slices and the juices from the pan poured over.

Variations

Crumbed liver Season the sliced liver with salt, pepper and lemon juice. Dip the slices first in lightly beaten egg and then in fine white breadcrumbs. Fry quickly in butter for about 3 minutes each side, then lift on to a hot serving dish. Add a little extra butter to the pan, 1 tablespoon of chopped parsley and a squeeze of lemon juice and pour over the liver.

French-style fried liver Cook the liver as before, omitting the aubergine. After cooking, lift the liver from the pan and pour off all but a tablespoon of the cooking oil. Add 1 small onion, finely chopped or minced, and fry gently for 2-3 minutes. Add a wine glass of dry white wine, raise the heat and boil quickly to reduce the liquid. Add 1 tablespoon of chopped parsley and pour over the liver.

Kidneys in sherry sauce

Serves 4
Cooking time about 10 minutes

METRIC
8 lambs' kidneys
50 g butter
1 medium-sized onion,
finely chopped
25 g flour
300 ml chicken stock
salt and freshly ground
pepper
2 tablespoons dry sherry
Garnish
chopped parsley

IMPERIAL
8 lambs' kidneys
2 oz butter
1 medium-sized onion,
finely chopped
1 oz flour
½ pint chicken stock
salt and freshly ground
pepper
2 tablespoons dry sherry
Garnish
chopped parsley

Using scissors, snip out the white core from each kidney, then pull away the thin covering of skin. Slice the kidney thinly. Melt half the butter in a frying pan. When hot add the kidneys and fry gently for 2-3 minutes. Remove the kidneys from the pan and keep hot. Add the remaining butter to the pan together with the chopped onion. Fry gently until the onion is tender and a little brown. Replace the kidneys in the pan and sprinkle with the flour. Stir to blend the flour in with the butter and then stir in the hot stock. Mix well and bring to the boil, stirring all the time. Simmer for about 5 minutes, still stirring. When no red juices flow from the kidneys they are cooked through; by this time too the sauce will be a rich brown. Check the seasoning and stir in the sherry. Serve with rice.

Pepper steak

Serves 4
Cooking time about 10 minutes

METRIC
rump steak, about 675 g, or
4 pieces frying steak
2 tablespoons whole black
peppercorns
50 g butter
4 tablespoons red wine

IMPERIAL
rump steak, about 1½ lb, or
4 pieces frying steak
2 tablespoons whole black
peppercorns
2 oz butter
4 tablespoons red wine

Trim the meat and set aside. Using a rolling pin or a heavy weight, crack the peppercorns coarsely and press into the surface of both sides of the meat. Brown quickly in hot butter on both sides, then lower the heat and cook for 10 minutes or until cooked to taste – see page 30. Lift the meat on to a hot serving dish and keep warm.

Add the red wine – allowing 1 table-spoon for each serving – to the hot juices in the pan. Heat through then pour over the meat and serve.
(*Illustrated on pages 46-47*)

Variation

Steak with soured cream Cook as directed above. Remove steak from the pan and keep warm. Stir in 1 (142-ml/5-fl oz) carton soured cream and heat just to boiling point. Season with salt and pepper and serve immediately along with the steak.

Steak with mustard sauce

Serves 4
Cooking time about 15 minutes

METRIC
4 fillet steaks
50 g butter
150 ml dry white wine
150 ml stock or use water plus stock cube
½ teaspoon salt
pinch of pepper
1 tablespoon French mustard
1 tablespoon dried tarragon

Trim the steaks. Heat the butter in a large frying pan, add the steaks and brown quickly on both sides. Reduce the heat and cook gently for 5-8 minutes according to taste. Remove from the pan on to a plate and keep warm.

Add the wine to the frying pan, bring to the boil, stirring all the time, and scraping the base of the pan well. Simmer rapidly until almost evaporated, then add the stock and seasoning and continue simmering until reduced by half — this takes about 5 minutes.

Meanwhile spread the steaks with a little of the mustard and sprinkle with the tarragon. Pour the sauce from the pan over the steaks and serve immediately.

IMPERIAL
4 fillet steaks
2 oz butter
¼ pint dry white wine
¼ pint stock or use water plus stock cube
½ teaspoon salt
pinch of pepper
1 tablespoon French mustard
1 tablespoon dried tarragon

Steak with onion sauce

Serves 4
Cooking time about 15 minutes

METRIC
1 piece rump steak about 675 g, cut 2·5-3·5 cm thick, or use frying steak
salt and pepper
75 g butter
450g onions, peeled and sliced
1 tablespoon vinegar
150 ml white wine or stock
1 tablespoon flour
2 tablespoons cream (optional)

Trim the steak and season with salt and pepper — it's best to keep the steak in one piece and cut before serving. Heat 50 g/ 2 oz of the butter in a large frying pan and add the steak. Fry quickly to brown on both sides, then add onions and lower heat. Cook for 8-12 minutes according to taste.

Lift the meat from the pan on to a hot serving dish and keep warm. Continue to cook the onions gently if necessary until soft then stir in the vinegar and white wine or stock. Season with salt and pepper and bring up to the boil. Cream the remaining butter with the flour and then add in small pieces to the onion sauce, stirring all the time until the sauce has thickened and re-boiled. Draw the pan off the heat, stir in the cream and spoon the sauce over the steak. Cut steak in portions and serve.

IMPERIAL
1 piece rump steak about 1½ lb, cut 1-1½ inches thick, or use frying steak
salt and pepper
3 oz butter
1 lb onions, peeled and sliced
1 tablespoon vinegar
¼ pint white wine or stock
1 tablespoon flour
2 tablespoons cream (optional)

Sautéed pork fillet with lemon

Serves 4
Cooking time 4-6 minutes

METRIC
1 small pork tenderloin, sometimes called pork fillet
seasoned flour
50 g butter
1 lemon

Trim any fat or sinew from the fillet and cut it into 3·5- or 5-cm/1½- or 2-inch thick slices. Beat each piece out until very thin. The easiest way is on a wet pastry board using a wet rolling pin; the water helps prevent the meat sticking or tearing.

Dip the thin pieces of pork fillet into the seasoned flour and then add to the hot butter in a frying pan. Fry gently for 2-3 minutes each side. Draw the pan off the heat and squeeze over the lemon juice. Serve at once with the juices from the pan.

IMPERIAL
1 small pork tenderloin, sometimes called pork fillet
seasoned flour
2 oz butter
1 lemon

Veal Parmesan

Serves 4
Cooking time 10 minutes

METRIC
4 veal escalopes
seasoned flour
1 egg, lightly beaten
50 g fresh white breadcrumbs
25 g grated Parmesan cheese
50 g butter
juice of ½ lemon
Garnish
parsley sprigs

Ask the butcher to beat the escalopes out. Dip in the seasoned flour. Then pass through the lightly beaten egg and finally coat both sides in the mixed breadcrumbs and Parmesan cheese. Fry in the hot butter for 10 minutes until brown on both sides, turning occasionally for even cooking. Lift the veal out on to a heated serving plate and keep warm.

Add the lemon juice to the hot butter and shake over the heat to mix. Strain over the veal and garnish with a sprig of parsley.

IMPERIAL
4 veal escalopes
seasoned flour
1 egg, lightly beaten
2 oz fresh white breadcrumbs
1 oz grated Parmesan cheese
2 oz butter
juice of ½ lemon
Garnish
parsley sprigs

Old-fashioned fried chicken

Serves 4
Cooking time 30 minutes

METRIC
4 chicken joints
seasoned flour
50-75 g butter
Garnish
parsley

IMPERIAL
4 chicken joints
seasoned flour
2-3 oz butter
Garnish
parsley

Wipe the chicken joints and trim away any loose pieces of skin. Dip in the seasoned flour to coat thoroughly and shake off excess flour.

Melt the butter in a heavy frying pan and add the chicken joints skin side downwards. Fry quickly to brown both sides of the joints. Then lower the heat, arrange the joints, skin side down again — the thickest fleshy part of the joints needs most cooking — and fry gently for 25 minutes in all. Turn occasionally for even cooking but allow most of the cooking time to the skin side of the bird. If liked, cover the pan with a lid to keep chicken joints moist, but remove pan lid for last 10 minutes of cooking time to allow joints to crisp and brown.

Serve with the juices from the pan and sprinkle with chopped parsley.

Variations

Spiced fried chicken Add 1 teaspoon curry powder or dry mustard to every 2 tablespoons flour; use for coating the chicken before frying.

Fried chicken with mushrooms Add 225 g/8 oz trimmed sliced button mushrooms about half way through the cooking time. Add more butter if necessary.

Fried chicken with onion and green pepper Peel and slice 1 large onion, halve and de-seed 1 green pepper. Shred the pepper finely and add to the chicken along with the onion about half way through the cooking time. Stir occasionally to cook the onion evenly. (*Illustrated opposite*)

Fried chicken with cream sauce When chicken is cooked, lift the joints from the pan and pour away all but 1 tablespoon of the drippings. Replace over the heat, stir in 1 tablespoon flour and then 300 ml/$\frac{1}{2}$ pint single cream and a generous seasoning of salt and pepper. Reheat until nearly boiling and add a squeeze of lemon juice, check the seasoning and serve over the chicken joints.

Overleaf — Pepper steak (see page 41)

Fried chicken with onion and green pepper (see above)

44

Scampi in cream and CURRY SAUCE

Serves 4
Cooking time about 10 minutes

METRIC
2 small onions
1 tablespoon olive oil
1 tablespoon curry powder
1 tablespoon flour
150 ml water
2 tablespoons tomato purée
1 tablespoon sweet chutney
or apricot jam
juice of $\frac{1}{2}$ lemon
450 g frozen scampi, thawed
25 g butter
3 tablespoons double cream

IMPERIAL
2 small onions
1 tablespoon olive oil
1 tablespoon curry powder
1 tablespoon flour
$\frac{1}{4}$ pint water
2 tablespoons tomato purée
1 tablespoon sweet chutney
or apricot jam
juice of $\frac{1}{2}$ lemon
1 lb frozen scampi, thawed
1 oz butter
3 tablespoons double cream

Peel and finely chop one of the onions. Heat the oil in a saucepan, add the onion and fry gently for about 5 minutes. Keep the pan covered so that the onion becomes tender but not brown. Stir in the curry powder and fry gently for a few moments to draw out the flavour. Stir in the flour. Gradually add the water and stir until the mixture comes to the boil. Add the tomato purée, chutney or jam and lemon juice. Simmer for about 5 minutes, then draw off the heat and strain the sauce.

Peel the remaining onion and chop finely. Heat the butter in a frying pan and add the onion. Fry gently to soften the onion, then add the prepared scampi. Toss the scampi in the hot butter for a few moments to heat through. The flesh will firm up and become slightly pink. Add the curry sauce and bring up to the boil. Stir in the cream, blend well and draw off the heat. Serve hot with buttered rice.

Trout meunière

Serves 4
Cooking time 5 minutes

METRIC
4 fresh trout
25 g flour
1 teaspoon salt
pinch of pepper
75 g butter
1 lemon
1 teaspoon chopped parsley

IMPERIAL
4 fresh trout
1 oz flour
1 teaspoon salt
pinch of pepper
3 oz butter
1 lemon
1 teaspoon chopped parsley

Ask the fishmonger to clean out the fish ready for cooking. Sift the flour, salt and pepper on to a plate. When ready to cook, roll the trout one at a time in the seasoned flour and add to 50 g/2 oz of the butter melted in a large frying pan.

Cook over a moderate heat for about 5 minutes, turning once. Lift out gently on to a hot serving dish. Pour away the over-browned butter and wipe out the pan with absorbent paper. Put in the remaining butter and allow to melt. Add the juice of half the lemon and the chopped parsley, heat for a moment then pour over the fish. Garnish with the remainder of the lemon cut in slices if liked.

(*Illustrated opposite*)

Trout meunière (see above)

FRiEd hERRiNGS iN OATMEAL

Serves 4
Cooking time 8 minutes

METRIC		IMPERIAL
4 herrings	Have the herrings cleaned and heads removed by the fishmonger. Split each herring open, place inside downwards on a clean working surface. Press down the back to loosen the bone, turn over and pull away the bone. Rinse the herrings under cold water and pat dry. Dip each one first in seasoned milk and then in the oatmeal, keeping the fish open flat. Pat the coating on firmly.	4 herrings
little milk		little milk
salt and pepper		salt and pepper
medium oatmeal		medium oatmeal
25 g butter		1 oz butter

Place the fish flesh side down in the hot butter and fry gently for about 4 minutes. Turn carefully to avoid breaking and cook on the second side. Serve.

EASY ONE-TWO-ONE METHOd fOR cookiNG RiCE

Rice is often an easy alternative to potato; there is little preparation and it cooks quickly. For savoury recipes always use the long-grain rice and follow these easy directions. Measures are easy to remember – 1 cup rice, 2 cups water, 1 teaspoon salt. Any cup will do, provided you use the same one for measuring both the rice and liquid. As a guide to quantities remember: 1 teacup rice equals 175 g/6 oz and 1 breakfast cup equals 225 g/8 oz.

Basic top-of-cooker method Put the rice, water and salt into a large saucepan. Bring up to the boil and stir once. Lower the heat, cover with a tight-fitting lid and simmer for about 15 minutes without removing the lid or stirring. Test the rice by biting a few grains and if not quite tender or if the liquid is not completely absorbed, replace the lid and cook for a few minutes longer. Remove from the heat, turn immediately into a serving dish and fluff lightly with a fork.

Oven method Put the rice and salt into an ovenproof casserole; add the boiling water and stir. Cover with a lid and cook in moderate oven (180°C, 350°F, Gas Mark 4) for about 40 minutes. Test as above and if the rice is not quite cooked or the water not absorbed, cover and cook for about 5 minutes more. Fluff the rice lightly with a fork and serve.

Fried rice This is an ideal way of cooking long-grain rice. Melt 25 g/1 oz butter in a large saucepan, add 1 finely chopped onion and stir in the rice. Fry over a moderate heat, stirring well, until golden brown. Add the boiling water or stock and salt. Bring up to the boil, stir once, cover with a tight-fitting lid, lower the heat and cook for 15 minutes without stirring, until the rice is tender and liquid absorbed. Fluff with a fork and serve.

Variations

Cheesy rice Add 50 g/2 oz grated Cheddar or Parmesan cheese and 15 g/½ oz butter; toss with a fork to mix. Serve with stews or casseroles.

Saffron rice Warm a good pinch of saffron in a small mixing basin, add a pinch of sugar and crush finely using the end of a rolling pin or wooden spoon. Add 1 tablespoon hot water and infuse for 1 minute. Strain the liquid into the cooked rice and toss with a fork until the grains of the rice have taken up the yellow colour. Serve with shellfish or veal.

Mint rice Add 3 tablespoons mint jelly and 15 g/½ oz butter to the cooked rice and using a fork, fold in until combined. Serve with grilled lamb chops.

Parsley rice Add 15 g/½ oz butter and 1 tablespoon finely chopped parsley to the cooked rice and toss to mix. Serve with stews, casseroles or curries.

Oriental rice Add about 2 tablespoons plumped seedless raisins — cover with boiling water for 1 minute then drain — and toss to mix. Serve with lamb or curry dishes.

Rice Lyonnaise

Serves 4
Cooking time 15 minutes

METRIC	IMPERIAL
25 g butter	1 oz butter
1 medium-sized onion, sliced	1 medium-sized onion, sliced
50 g button mushrooms, cleaned	2 oz button mushrooms, cleaned
1 (425-g) can tomatoes	1 (15-oz) can tomatoes
1 teaspoon salt	1 teaspoon salt
1 small green pepper, de-seeded and finely chopped	1 small green pepper, de-seeded and finely chopped
1 small red pepper, de-seeded and finely chopped	1 small red pepper, de-seeded and finely chopped
2 teaspoons castor sugar	2 teaspoons castor sugar
175-225 g rice, cooked (see page 50)	6-8 oz rice, cooked (see page 50)
25 g grated Parmesan cheese	1 oz grated Parmesan cheese

Melt the butter in a saucepan, add the onion and mushrooms and fry gently until soft and golden. Stir in the contents of the can of tomatoes, plus the liquid from the can, salt, peppers, sugar and cooked rice. Cover with a lid and simmer for 15 minutes. Remove the pan lid towards the end of the cooking time to allow the excess moisture to evaporate. Fork up the rice mixture and sprinkle with Parmesan cheese. Serve with chops, steaks and hamburgers.

Spanish rice

Serves 4
Cooking time about 20 minutes

METRIC	IMPERIAL
25 g butter	1 oz butter
1 small onion, peeled and finely chopped	1 small onion, peeled and finely chopped
225 g long-grain rice	8 oz long-grain rice
600 ml chicken stock made with a cube	1 pint chicken stock made with a cube

Melt the butter in a frying pan, add the onion and fry gently for 5 minutes until soft and beginning to brown. Add the rice and mix into the butter and onion. Add the hot stock and bring to a simmer. Cover and cook over a low heat until the stock is absorbed and the rice is tender, about 20 minutes. Fluff up the rice with a fork and serve with hamburgers, meat loaf or sausages.

Minute savers

Garlic burns quickly. In a recipe where garlic and onion are fried, first fry the onion until soft then add the garlic and fry only a further few moments.

Pour hot fat from frying or grilling into an empty used can and allow to solidify before throwing out – that is unless you wish to keep it for another time.

A container of ready mixed seasoned flour is handy for coating foods to be fried. Make up in advance by sifting 100 g/4 oz flour with 4 teaspoons salt and 2 teaspoons ground pepper. Use as required.

Where seasoned flour is used for coating chicken joints or liver or meat for frying, keep any left over and use for thickening a sauce in the pan.

Make up your own mixed seasoning and use it for all general flavouring particularly sauces, soups and casseroles. Sift together three times, 225 g/8 oz salt, 1 tablespoon ground white pepper and 1 teaspoon ground mace. These quantities are a perfectly balanced blend of flavours.

Dip chicken joints in beaten egg and then in a packet of breadcrumb stuffing mix. Excellent for baked or fried chicken, adds extra flavour too.

Crush cornflakes or biscuits in a roomy polythene bag. This keeps them in one place with no mess to clear up afterwards. Some cooks like to use the same idea for flouring chicken joints. Put the flour and seasoning in a polythene bag. Add the chicken joints which can be shaken until evenly coated.

Butter gives the best flavour for shallow frying of meat, chicken or fish. A little oil heated along with the butter takes away nothing of the taste but does help prevent butter from scorching and browning too quickly at a high temperature.

To make an egg go further for coating fish, chicken joints or veal escalopes for frying – add 1 tablespoon oil and beat.

Always pass a slice of white bread through the machine after mincing ingredients for a pâté or meat loaf; it pushes out the last few pieces of meat or liver that always remain inside.

Sprinkle a chopping board or rolling pin with cold water before beating out escalopes thinly or moisten the palms of your hands with water before shaping meat balls or hamburgers. Remember that water, not flour, is the medium here that prevents sticking.

Use the blade of a knife and the corner of a vegetable chopping board to crush garlic to a cream with salt and draw the juices. Then the garlic blends and flavours evenly with no pieces to bite on.

Use oven-to-table ware when possible. Clean any cooking stains from the dishes before setting on the table, using the wet corner of a teacloth and salt as an abrasive.

SNACK MEALS

In the evening, simple snack meals make less work for the cook. Toast snacks, cheese or egg | dishes all make nourishing meals.

Devilled roe savoury

Serves 4
Cooking time 5 minutes

METRIC		IMPERIAL
175 g fresh soft herring roes	Separate the herring roes. Sift together the flour, curry powder and a seasoning of salt and pepper, toss the roes in this and then fry very gently in the melted butter for a few minutes only each side. Add a dash of Worcestershire sauce to the pan along with the lemon juice. Cook for a further minute, shaking the pan to flavour the roes. Serve the roes on hot toast, garnished with a sprig of parsley.	6 oz fresh soft herring roes
1 tablespoon flour		1 tablespoon flour
1 teaspoon curry powder		1 teaspoon curry powder
salt and pepper		salt and pepper
25 g butter		1 oz butter
dash of Worcestershire sauce		dash of Worcestershire sauce
squeeze of lemon juice		squeeze of lemon juice
4 slices hot buttered toast		4 slices hot buttered toast

Fried ham and cheese sandwiches

Serves 4
Cooking time about 5 minutes

METRIC		IMPERIAL
8 thin slices white bread, with crusts removed	On four of the bread slices arrange a slice each of ham and cheese. Top with a second slice of bread.	8 thin slices white bread, with crusts removed
4 slices ham	Fry the sandwiches in plenty of hot butter. When beginning to brown, turn and fry the second side. Turn several times, adding more butter if necessary, and cook until golden brown and crisp.	4 slices ham
4 slices Gruyère cheese		4 slices Gruyère cheese
50-75 g butter for frying	Cut in half diagonally and serve.	2-3 oz butter for frying

Savoury rarebit

Serves 4
Cooking time about 5 minutes

METRIC		IMPERIAL
25 g butter	Heat the butter in a saucepan and add the onion. Fry gently over low heat until onion is soft and a little brown. Add the cheese and stir until melted, then add the milk and a seasoning of salt and pepper and stir until well blended. Draw the pan off the heat. Top each slice of toast with two grilled bacon rashers. Spread the rarebit over the toast and garnish with a slice of tomato. Place under a preheated hot grill for a few minutes or until bubbling hot and brown. Serve at once.	1 oz butter
½ small onion, finely chopped		½ small onion, finely chopped
175 g Cheddar cheese, grated		6 oz Cheddar cheese, grated
2 tablespoons milk		2 tablespoons milk
salt and pepper		salt and pepper
4 slices toast		4 slices toast
8 back bacon rashers		8 back bacon rashers
1 tomato		1 tomato

CORN FRITTERS WITH bacon

Serves 4
Cooking time about 15 minutes

METRIC
1 (312-g) can whole kernel sweetcorn
salt and pepper
1 egg
1½ tablespoons flour
50-75 g butter for frying
8 bacon rashers

IMPERIAL
1 (11-oz) can whole kernel sweetcorn
salt and pepper
1 egg
1½ tablespoons flour
2-3 oz butter for frying
8 bacon rashers

Drain the liquid from the can of sweetcorn and empty the corn into a bowl. Season well with salt and pepper, then stir in the egg and flour and, using a wooden spoon, mix to a creamy batter.

Heat some of the butter in a pan and add dessertspoons of the sweetcorn batter. Fry over a moderate heat until browned on one side, then flip over and brown the second side. Add more butter as necessary to fry all the fritters (this mixture makes about eight). Keep the fritters warm and fry the trimmed bacon rashers quickly, then serve both together. Corn fritters are delicious with fried chicken joints.

SAUTÉED kidney with bacon

Serves 4
Cooking time about 5 minutes

METRIC
8 lambs' kidneys
seasoned flour
4 back bacon rashers
1 tablespoon chopped parsley
4 thin slices white bread
butter for spreading

IMPERIAL
8 lambs' kidneys
seasoned flour
4 back bacon rashers
1 tablespoon chopped parsley
4 thin slices white bread
butter for spreading

Halve the kidneys, snip out the core using a pair of scissors, and roll the kidneys in seasoned flour. Trim and chop the bacon rashers and fry lightly. Drain the bacon from the pan and add the kidneys to the hot bacon fat. Fry gently for about 5 minutes. Add the chopped parsley and bacon and reheat gently. Toast the bread slices and butter. Pile the kidneys and bacon mixture on top; serve at once.

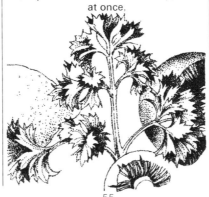

Curried prawns with EGG

Serves 4
Cooking time about 6 minutes

METRIC
8 eggs
150 ml milk
salt and pepper
25 g butter or margarine
1 tablespoon curry powder
1 (200-g) can prawns
4 slices buttered toast
Garnish
chopped parsley

Crack the eggs into a mixing bowl. Add the milk, and a generous seasoning of salt and pepper and beat well to mix.

Heat the butter in a medium-sized saucepan, add the curry powder and prawns and heat through gently for 5 minutes. Add the beaten egg mixture and stir over low heat until the egg begins to cook and thicken. Draw the pan off the heat while the mixture is still moist — take care not to over-cook, and dividing the mixture equally, spoon on to the hot toast and sprinkle with chopped parsley.

IMPERIAL
8 eggs
$\frac{1}{4}$ pint milk
salt and pepper
1 oz butter or margarine
1 tablespoon curry powder
1 (7-oz) can prawns
4 slices buttered toast
Garnish
chopped parsley

Creamed mushrooms

ON TOAST

Serves 4
Cooking time 6 minutes

METRIC
25 g butter
225 g fresh button mushrooms trimmed and sliced
$\frac{1}{2}$ teaspoon salt
freshly ground pepper
2 tablespoons flour
300 ml creamy milk
juice of $\frac{1}{2}$ lemon
4 slices buttered toast

Melt the butter, add the mushrooms and fry quickly over a fairly high heat, stirring all the time. Do not over-cook the mushrooms — they should only be fried for 1 minute. Add the salt and pepper and sprinkle over the flour. Stir to blend then gradually stir in the milk and bring up to simmering. Squeeze over the lemon juice and draw the pan off the heat. Spoon the mushrooms over the hot toast slices and serve.

IMPERIAL
1 oz butter
8 oz fresh button mushrooms, trimmed and sliced
$\frac{1}{2}$ teaspoon salt
freshly ground pepper
2 tablespoons flour
$\frac{1}{2}$ pint creamy milk
juice of $\frac{1}{2}$ lemon
4 slices buttered toast

Variation
Sherried mushrooms Follow the recipe above, adding a pinch of dried mixed herbs with the flour. Stir in 150 ml/$\frac{1}{4}$ pint single cream, 1 teaspoon English mustard and 1 tablespoon sherry. Heat until simmering then spoon over hot toast slices and garnish with chopped parsley. (*Illustrated opposite*)

Sherried mushrooms (see above)

Quick egg dishes

There are a hundred and one ways to serve eggs for quick meals. Eggs blend well with new young vegetables, sharp or mild cheese, crisp bacon or fresh herbs. They make featherlight soufflé omelettes, delicious served with a savoury sauce, flat Spanish omelettes with onion, tomato or green pepper, or scrambled egg.

Omelettes Puffy or soufflé omelettes look glamorous enough to serve to your guests, while the flat open omelettes can be made really filling, using your own choice of vegetables or meat, with added herbs and seasonings.

Tossed salads go well with any omelette and in particular the soufflé ones. Try a salad of washed lettuce, tomato, cucumber slices and watercress sprigs — add a little crispness with shredded green pepper or chicory and toss in oil and vinegar dressing. On the other hand, flat omelettes are nice with a hot vegetable, say beans, plain or in a white sauce, peas with fried bacon or onion added, buttered carrots with chopped parsley, sliced fried mushrooms, or with whole kernel sweetcorn stirred in.

Soufflé omelette

Serves 2
Cooking time 6 minutes

METRIC		IMPERIAL
3 eggs		3 eggs
1 tablespoon hot water		1 tablespoon hot water
salt and pepper		salt and pepper
25 g butter for frying		1 oz butter for frying
Garnish		*Garnish*
cheese or parsley		cheese or parsley

Separate the egg yolks and whites, putting the whites in a small bowl and the yolks into a large one. For best results, warm the larger bowl — fill with hot water for 5 minutes before using, then the egg yolks will whisk up more quickly. Add the hot water and a good seasoning of salt and pepper to the yolks and whisk until light in colour and thick.

Quickly beat the egg whites until stiff, then, using a metal spoon, gently fold into the egg yolk mixture.

Heat the butter in a 20- or 23-cm/8- or 9-inch omelette or frying pan until bubbling hot. Pour in the omelette mixture and spread evenly over the pan. Leave over a low heat to cook gently for 5 minutes, until the omelette is puffy and almost cooked through and brown on the underside. Remove from the heat and place under a moderate grill for only 1 minute — just to cook the top surface. If a very soft omelette is preferred omit this stage. Slip a palette knife under one side of the omelette and fold over on to the other. Hold for a few seconds to seal the two halves together then lift out on to a hot serving plate. Cut in half and serve plain, topped with grated cheese or chopped parsley or one of the following sauces.

Prawn salad (see page 71)

Creole sauce for soufflé omelette

Serves 4
Cooking time 30 minutes

Add the prepared onion, green pepper and crushed garlic to the hot oil in a saucepan. Fry gently for 5 minutes to soften the vegetables but do not brown. Stir in the remaining ingredients and bring up to the boil. Cover with a lid, reduce the heat and simmer for 30 minutes.

Remove the bay leaf and serve.

METRIC
2 onions, peeled and sliced
2 green peppers, de-seeded and shredded
1 clove of garlic, crushed with salt
2 tablespoons cooking oil
1 (425-g) can tomatoes
1 bay leaf
½ teaspoon dried thyme
salt
little freshly ground pepper

IMPERIAL
2 onions, peeled and sliced
2 green peppers, de-seeded and shredded
1 clove of garlic, crushed with salt
2 tablespoons cooking oil
1 (15-oz) can tomatoes
1 bay leaf
½ teaspoon dried thyme
salt
little freshly ground pepper

Onion Sauce for soufflé omelette

Serves 2
Cooking time about 15 minutes

Heat the butter in a medium-sized saucepan and then stir in the onions. Cover with a lid and cook slowly for 10 minutes, then remove the lid and cook quickly until the onions are begining to turn golden brown. Stir in the flour and cook over the heat for about 1 minute, before adding the stock and the milk. Bring to the boil stirring all the time and simmer for 1-2 minutes; add salt, freshly ground pepper to taste and a little chopped parsley. Serve.

METRIC
50 g butter
2 onions, peeled and sliced
25 g plain flour
300 ml stock or use water plus chicken stock cube
150 ml milk
seasoning
chopped parsley

IMPERIAL
2 oz butter
2 onions, peeled and sliced
1 oz plain flour
½ pint stock or use water plus chicken stock cube
¼ pint milk
seasoning
chopped parsley

Open omelettes The bulky, flat open omelette makes a marvellous meal. Almost any combination of ingredients may be used, these being heated through in the pan before the omelette mixture is added. The omelette can be turned and browned on the underside or flashed under a moderate grill. It is always served flat. Unless serving a single omelette, cook sufficient for two in a large frying pan and serve it cut in half.

Onion and potato omelette

Serves 2
Cooking time about 15 minutes

METRIC
4 eggs
1 tablespoon water
salt and pepper
pinch of dried thyme
1 tablespoon chopped parsley
25 g butter
1 large onion, sliced
2 medium potatoes, peeled and diced

IMPERIAL
4 eggs
1 tablespoon water
salt and pepper
pinch of dried thyme
1 tablespoon chopped parsley
1 oz butter
1 large onion, sliced
2 medium potatoes, peeled and diced

Crack the eggs into a bowl, add the water and a generous seasoning of salt and pepper. Beat well to mix; add the thyme and parsley and set aside.

Melt the butter in a 20- or 23-cm/8- or 9-inch frying pan, add the onion and potatoes and fry gently over a low heat until the potatoes are cooked and the onion is soft — this takes about 10 minutes. Season with salt, otherwise the finished omelette could taste a little dull.

Add the beaten egg mixture all at once, and using a fork, stir the mixture until beginning to thicken. Stop stirring and allow the underside to brown. Flash quickly under a moderate grill for about 1 minute to set the top of the omelette. Cut in half and serve.

Spanish omelette

Serves 2
Cooking time about 15 minutes

METRIC
4 eggs
1 tablespoon water
salt and pepper
squeeze of lemon juice
25 g butter or 1 tablespoon salad oil
1 onion, sliced
1 green pepper, de-seeded and shredded
2 tomatoes

IMPERIAL
4 eggs
1 tablespoon water
salt and pepper
squeeze of lemon juice
1 oz butter or 1 tablespoon salad oil
1 onion, sliced
1 green pepper, de-seeded and shredded
2 tomatoes

Crack the eggs into a bowl, add the water, a generous seasoning of salt and pepper and the lemon juice. Beat well to mix; set aside.

Heat the butter or oil in a 20- or 23-cm/8- or 9-inch frying pan. Add the onion and green pepper and fry gently until both are soft — this takes about 10 minutes. Meanwhile nick the skins of the tomatoes and plunge into boiling water for 1 minute. Drain, peel away the skins and slice. Add the tomatoes to the cooked onion mixture then stir in the beaten egg. Using a fork stir the mixture gently in the pan; stirring continuously helps the egg to thicken evenly. When the mixture is beginning to set, stop stirring and allow the underside of the omelette to brown. Turn over using a palette knife or fish slice and brown quickly on the second side. Do not overcook; an omelette is nicest a little soft. Cut in half and serve at once.

Anchovy and tomato omelette

Serves 2
Cooking time about 5 minutes

METRIC		IMPERIAL
4 eggs		4 eggs
1 tablespoon water		1 tablespoon water
salt and pepper		salt and pepper
6 tomatoes		6 tomatoes
,1 tablespoon finely chopped anchovies		1 tablespoon finely chopped anchovies
25 g butter		1 oz butter
Garnish		*Garnish*
chopped parsley		chopped parsley

Crack the eggs into a bowl, add the water and a generous seasoning of salt and pepper. Beat well to mix, then set aside.

Nick the skins of the tomatoes and plunge into boiling water for 1 minute. Drain and peel away the skins. (When adding tomatoes to an omelette it is better to remove the skins first; the appearance of the tomatoes is improved since any skins curl up while cooking and spoil the appearance of the finished dish.) Slice the tomatoes thickly and set aside along with the anchovies.

Melt the butter in a 20- or 23-cm/8- or 9-inch frying pan and when hot add the egg mixture all at once. Using a fork stir quickly until the mixture has thickened and is beginning to set. Stop stirring and allow the underside to brown. Before the egg mixture has set completely, sprinkle the surface with the chopped anchovies and then arrange the slices of tomato all over the top. Flash under a moderate grill for about 1 minute to cook the surface; sprinkle with parsley then cut in half and serve at once without turning.

Country omelette

Serves 2
Cooking time about 15 minutes

METRIC		IMPERIAL
4 eggs		4 eggs
1 tablespoon water		1 tablespoon water
salt and pepper		salt and pepper
25 g butter		1 oz butter
4 bacon rashers		4 bacon rashers
1 small onion, peeled and cut in rings		1 small onion, peeled and cut in rings
sliced cooked potato (optional)		sliced cooked potato (optional)

Crack the eggs into a bowl; add the water and salt and pepper. Beat well to mix, then set aside.

Heat the butter in a 20- or 23-cm/8- or 9-inch frying pan. Add the trimmed and chopped bacon rashers, the onion rings and potato if used. Fry gently until bacon is crisp and onion and potato are browned. Pour the egg mixture over the vegetables and stir gently with a fork. When the mixture begins to set, stop stirring and allow the underside of the omelette to brown. Turn the omelette and brown quickly on the second side. Serve at once sliced in half with a mixed salad.

Scrambled eggs

A more sensible and quicker way to cook scrambled eggs is to use a large frying pan.

Prepare a basic omelette mixture using 8-9 eggs which will be sufficient for 4 servings.

Scrambled egg with herbs

Serves 4
Cooking time about 4 minutes

METRIC
9 eggs
150 ml milk
1 teaspoon salt
freshly ground pepper
3 tablespoons finely chopped parsley
2 teaspoons finely chopped chives
25 g butter

IMPERIAL
9 eggs
¼ pint milk
1 teaspoon salt
freshly ground pepper
3 tablespoons finely chopped parsley
2 teaspoons finely chopped chives
1 oz butter

Crack the eggs into a mixing bowl, add the milk and seasoning and beat well to mix. Add the chopped herbs.

Heat the butter in a frying pan over a low heat and when melted, but not brown, pour in the egg mixture. Cook over a low heat, stirring most of the time. Use a metal spoon rather than a wooden spoon; this way the mixture does not break up so much. Draw the pan off the heat when the mixture is thickened but still moist and not dry. Serve at once.

Variations

With curry Prepare the basic mixture, omitting the herbs, but add 1½ teaspoons curry powder. Cook as above.

With ham Prepare the basic mixture, omitting the herbs. Add 100 g/4 oz finely chopped ham to the butter before the egg mixture. Heat through gently then stir in the egg mixture; cook as above.

Devilled scrambled Egg

Serves 4
Cooking time about 4 minutes

METRIC
8 eggs
150 ml single cream
1 teaspoon salt
pinch of pepper
1 teaspoon dry mustard
½ teaspoon Worcestershire sauce
75 g butter
225 g button mushrooms, trimmed and sliced

IMPERIAL
8 eggs
¼ pint single cream
1 teaspoon salt
pinch of pepper
1 teaspoon dry mustard
½ teaspoon Worcestershire sauce
3 oz butter
8 oz button mushrooms, trimmed and sliced

Crack the eggs into a mixing bowl, add the cream, salt, pepper, mustard and Worcestershire sauce. Beat well to mix and set aside. Heat half the butter in a frying pan over low heat. Strain in the egg mixture and stir over a moderate heat, stirring until the mixture begins to thicken but is still moist. Meanwhile fry the mushrooms separately in the remaining butter. Draw the pan off the heat and serve the scrambled eggs along with the mushrooms.

Egg and mushroom scramble

Serves 4
Cooking time about 5 minutes

METRIC
1 (298-g) can cream of mushroom soup
8 eggs
freshly ground black pepper
25 g butter
Garnish
chopped parsley

Empty the contents of the can of soup into a mixing bowl and stir until smooth. Crack the eggs into the bowl and add a seasoning of pepper. Whisk well until blended.

Melt the butter in a large frying pan over a low heat. Pour in the mushroom mixture and cook gently, stirring occasionally, until the mixture has thickened and is beginning to set. Sprinkle with parsley and serve with hot toast.

IMPERIAL
1 (10½-oz) can cream of mushroom soup
8 eggs
freshly ground black pepper
1 oz butter
Garnish
chopped parsley

Variations

Vegetable scramble Follow the recipe above, using 1 (298-g/10½-oz) can of cream of vegetable soup.

Chicken scramble Follow the recipe above, using 1 (298-g/10½-oz) can of cream of chicken soup.

Celery scramble Follow the recipe above, using 1 (298-g/10½-oz) can of cream of celery soup.

Minute savers

It's worth buying a non-stick frying pan or saucepan just for scrambled eggs — it saves a good deal of difficult cleaning afterwards.

Never plunge eggs cold from the refrigerator into boiling water — it's a sure way of cracking them. Cover them with cold water and bring up to the boil, then cook as required. Or try using a commercial 'egg pick' to puncture the shell and prevent cracking.

Sprinkle paprika pepper over cheese, or cheese sauce-topped snacks, before grilling — it browns beautifully and instantly.

To get rid of the very salty flavour in anchovy fillets, soak them in milk about 30 minutes before using.

Always heat any cooked filling to be added to an omelette. Onion, bacon, mushrooms, ham or cooked potato should be fried or heated gently in butter first.

When poaching eggs, add 1 teaspoon vinegar to the water before cooking — it helps the white of the egg coagulate quickly and keep a better shape.

To retain the maximum volume in a hot soufflé recipe, always fold a little of the beaten egg whites into the mixture first to lighten the texture before folding in the remainder.

Egg whites do not whisk up foamy and stiff if they contain any trace of egg yolk. As an extra precaution a chef always wipes the inside of a mixing bowl with the cut surface of a lemon to remove any traces of grease. A pinch of salt helps to give a better volume too.

1 tablespoon of oil added to the salted water for cooking pasta will keep large pieces like lasagne and canneloni from sticking together. Oil also helps to prevent the water from frothing up and boiling over, so add to the water for cooking spaghetti and macaroni too.

Salads and dressings

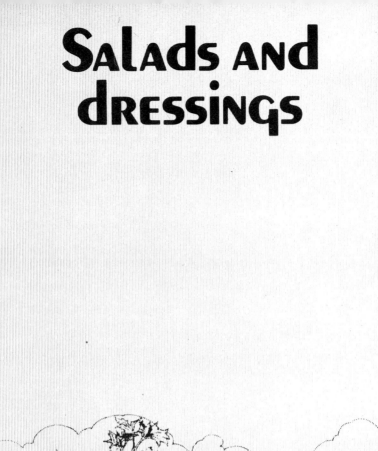

A salad can be a collection of almost any fresh salad vegetables, cold meats, fish, cheese or eggs that you care to put together. Presentation, colour and appearance are very important – a salad should look fresh, colourful and appetising. Salad dressings make all the difference to vegetables and relishes or pickles give zest to cold meats.

The preparation of salad vegetables is important and care should be taken to preserve their freshness. Never store prepared salad vegetables uncovered in the refrigerator; keep fresh either in plastic containers with sealed lids or in closed polythene bags.

Lettuce and curly endive Select crisp fresh heads and wash in plenty of cold water. The best way is to dunk the head up and down in cold water to draw out all the dirt. Break apart and separate the leaves, tear lettuce into smaller pieces if liked but never cut it with a knife. Shake the leaves in a colander or salad basket, or pat dry in a clean tea towel. Choose from round lettuces or the long, crisp cos variety.

Chicory Cut a thin slice from the base of the chicory then wash the heads under cold water. Shake dry. Discard any bruised outer leaves and cut across in 1-cm/½-inch pieces then separate out the layers.

Celery Separate the stalks from the head of celery and scrub clean; trim off the base and tops and then shred finely.

Leeks Trim off the base and top green part leaving on the white stalk and about 2·5 cm/ 1 inch of the green part. Cut lengthwise with a knife to the centre only and then wash under cold running water to remove all grit. Shred finely.

Tomatoes Wash and cut into slices or quarters. Or cut into attractive tomato lilies by making zig-zag cuts round the middle of each tomato with a sharp knife; separate into two neat halves. Sliced tomatoes with chopped spring onions or chives are delicious in oil and vinegar dressing.

Radishes Wash thoroughly and trim off the tops and tails. Add to a salad sliced or whole. Or make pretty radish roses – using a small sharp knife slit the radish down from the tail end about four or six times to form petals. Take care not to cut right through. Leave in iced water to open out.

Cucumber Wash thoroughly and peel thinly, or flute the skin by running the prongs of a fork down the length. Slice thinly across.

Cress, watercress and chives Wash very thoroughly under running water. Use the tops of cress and watercress only; snip off cress with scissors and using your fingers pinch off the upper parts of watercress. Pick out the greenest leaves of chives and chop finely.

Garlic Only the merest suspicion should be used in salads. The best way is to crush the clove and rub it around the inside of the salad bowl or dish, then discard the clove.

Carrots Scrub to remove any dirt. Always use new, young carrots cut into thin matchsticks or finely grated. Alternatively pare off very thin layers lengthwise to make carrot curls. Leave them in iced water to go crisp.

Beetroot Buy them already cooked; slide off the skins using your forefinger and thumb and slice or dice the flesh. Serve separately in vinegar or add it to the salad just before serving as the colour quickly stains the other salad vegetables.

Mushrooms Select small cultivated button mushrooms. Wipe and trim the ends of the stalks. Slice thinly downwards and use raw.

Onions Ordinary onions should be peeled and sliced into rings. Cover with vinegar for several hours before using – this way they crisp up nicely.

Spring onions should be well washed, then you should trim off the roots and top parts of the green. Use whole or slice into rings.

Green peppers Slice them in half lengthwise. Remove the seeds and core then shred flesh and use it raw.

Salads

Simple salads can be made up very quickly using sliced cold meat, ham or tongue, sliced cooked chicken or chicken joints, smoked sausages such as salami, or fish such as herring rollmops, canned or fresh cooked salmon, lobster, crab or tuna or cheese or eggs.

Garnish with sliced tomato, crisp lettuce hearts, sliced cucumber, sprigs of watercress or sliced or quartered hard-boiled eggs. Serve with a vegetable or rice salad separately.

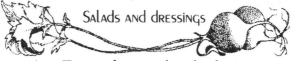

Tossed mixed salad

Serves 4

METRIC
1 lettuce
½ cucumber
3 tomatoes
oil and vinegar dressing (see page 72)

Wash the lettuce discarding the outer bruised leaves and shake dry. Peel and thinly slice the cucumber and either slice or quarter the tomatoes. Just before serving toss in the prepared dressing. Any number of other ingredients may be added such as chicory, watercress, shredded green pepper or quartered hard-boiled egg.

IMPERIAL
1 lettuce
½ cucumber
3 tomatoes
oil and vinegar dressing (see page 72)

Old-fashioned egg salad

Serves 4
Cooking time 5-8 minutes

METRIC
1 lettuce heart
6 eggs
1 large onion, thinly sliced
1 teaspoon salt
freshly ground pepper
2 tablespoons vinegar
4 tablespoons oil
1 teaspoon Worcestershire sauce
1 tablespoon finely chopped parsley
2 tablespoons grated Cheddar cheese

Wash the lettuce heart and break into leaves. Arrange the leaves over the base of a salad bowl. Cover the eggs with cold water and bring up to the boil. Boil gently for 5-8 minutes then plunge the eggs into cold water and remove the shells. Slice when cold and arrange over the lettuce in layers with the onion.

Combine the salt, pepper, vinegar, oil, Worcestershire sauce, parsley and cheese in a bowl. Pour over the salad and serve.

This salad is nice with sliced ham, cold sliced beef or cooked chicken joints.

IMPERIAL
1 lettuce heart
6 eggs
1 large onion, thinly sliced
1 teaspoon salt
freshly ground pepper
2 tablespoons vinegar
4 tablespoons oil
1 teaspoon Worcestershire sauce
1 tablespoon finely chopped parsley
2 tablespoons grated Cheddar cheese

Scandinavian cucumber salad

Serves 4-6

METRIC
1 medium cucumber
salt
1 tablespoon castor sugar
1 tablespoon wine vinegar
4 tablespoons cold water
freshly ground pepper
Garnish
chopped parsley

Wash the cucumber then slice very thinly with a sharp knife. Layer the slices in a bowl with salt. Leave for 1 hour for the salt to extract the juices. Meanwhile in a glass serving bowl, mix the sugar, vinegar, water and pepper. Now rinse the cucumber slices, drain well and add to the pickling liquid. Sprinkle with chopped parsley and serve.

This salad is nice with cold meats, particularly beef, lamb, chicken or ham. A fork is useful for lifting out the slices.

IMPERIAL
1 medium cucumber
salt
1 tablespoon castor sugar
1 tablespoon wine vinegar
4 tablespoons cold water
freshly ground pepper
Garnish
chopped parsley

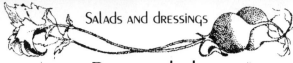

Potato salad

Serves 4-6
Cooking time 15-20 minutes

METRIC
450 g new potatoes
1 small clove of garlic
4 spring onions
2 tablespoons finely chopped parsley
salt and freshly ground pepper
3-4 tablespoons mayonnaise
3 tablespoons single cream
Garnish
few crisp lettuce leaves
chopped chives

IMPERIAL
1 lb new potatoes
1 small clove of garlic
4 spring onions
2 tablespoons finely chopped parsley
salt and freshly ground pepper
3-4 tablespoons mayonnaise
3 tablespoons single cream
Garnish
few crisp lettuce leaves
chopped chives

Scrub the potatoes and cook in their skins in gently boiling water until just tender — take care not to over-cook, otherwise they break up on slicing. Drain, cool a little and peel off the skins. Cut into neat cubes. Rub a bowl with the garlic, then add the potato. Add the sliced spring onions, parsley and a good seasoning of salt and pepper. Thin the mayonnaise down with the cream and add to the potato, mixing the ingredients while the potatoes are still warm so that they absorb maximum flavour. Leave until quite cold then spoon into a salad bowl lined with the lettuce leaves, sprinkle with a few freshly chopped chives and serve.

Serve with cold meat, chicken, ham or herring rollmops.

Soused herrings

Serves 4
Cooking time 40-45 minutes

METRIC
4 herrings, with heads removed
150 ml vinegar
150 ml water
few peppercorns
1 bay leaf
½ onion, sliced into rings

IMPERIAL
4 herrings, with heads removed
¼ pint vinegar
¼ pint water
few peppercorns
1 bay leaf
½ onion, sliced into rings

Wash the herrings under cold water and scrape away any loose scales with a knife. Trim off the fins with scissors and cut off the tails. Slit the herrings lengthwise and remove the roes.

Place each herring in turn, cut side down, on a clean working surface and press sharply down the backbone to loosen. Turn over and carefully pull away the bone.

Roll up the fillets and place, packed closely together, in a 0·75-litre/1-1½-pint pie dish. Mix together the vinegar and water and pour over the herrings. Add the peppercorns, bay leaf and onion rings. Cover with greased paper or a lid and cook in a moderate oven (180°C, 350°F, Gas Mark 4) for 40-45 minutes. Allow to cool in the liquid, then drain and garnish with a few of the onion rings.

Serve with a tossed green salad or potato salad and fresh lettuce.

Coleslaw salad

Serves 6

METRIC
½ white cabbage heart
2-3 new young carrots
2 dessert apples
1-2 sticks celery
4-5 tablespoons oil and
vinegar dressing (see
page 72)
4 tablespoons mayonnaise
3 tablespoons single cream

Rinse the cabbage under cold water and remove any outer damaged leaves. Cut in half, cut away the core and then shred the cabbage finely. Place in a large mixing bowl and add the scrubbed and coarsely grated carrots, the apples, peeled, quartered and coarsely grated, and the scrubbed and finely shredded celery. Toss the salad with oil and vinegar dressing; leave to chill for 15-20 minutes.

Meanwhile in a small bowl thin down the mayonnaise with the cream. Pour over the salad and toss well to mix before serving.

IMPERIAL
½ white cabbage heart
2-3 new young carrots
2 dessert apples
1-2 sticks celery
4-5 tablespoons oil and
vinegar dressing (see
page 72)
4 tablespoons mayonnaise
3 tablespoons single cream

Onions in soured cream

Serves 4

METRIC
2 medium onions
1 (142-ml) carton soured
cream
¼ teaspoon salt
1 teaspoon lemon juice

Peel the onions leaving them whole. Slice into rings and place in a mixing bowl. Cover with boiling water and allow to soak for 2 minutes. Drain and chill.

Meanwhile combine together the soured cream, salt and lemon juice. Add the onion rings and toss well to mix. Chill until ready to serve.

This salad is nice with any cold meats or fish.

IMPERIAL
2 medium onions
1 (5-fl oz) carton soured
cream
¼ teaspoon salt
1 teaspoon lemon juice

Celery and tomato salad

Serves 4

METRIC
1 small head of celery
2 leeks
4 tomatoes
1 box cress
oil and vinegar dressing (see
page 72)

Remove the stalks from the head of celery, scrub well and shred. Trim and wash the leeks, shred finely and mix with the celery. Pile this over the centre of a large flat plate. Slice the tomatoes and arrange around the edge. Wash and snip the tops off the cress and tuck around the edge of the plate, under the tomato slices.

Prepare the dressing and, when ready to serve, give it a final mix and spoon over the salad.

IMPERIAL
1 small head of celery
2 leeks
4 tomatoes
1 box cress
oil and vinegar dressing (see
page 72)

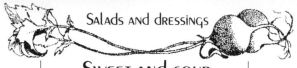

Sweet and sour
TOMATOES

Serves 6-8

METRIC
1·5 kg tomatoes
4 tablespoons wine or malt vinegar
3 tablespoons water
1 tablespoon castor sugar
1 small onion, finely chopped
freshly ground pepper

Nick the skins on the tomatoes and plunge them into boiling water for 1 minute, drain, then peel off the skins. Slice the tomatoes and arrange in a serving dish.

Mix together vinegar, water, sugar and onion and pour over the tomatoes. Leave to stand in the refrigerator. Sprinkle with the pepper and serve with cold meats.

IMPERIAL
3 lb tomatoes
4 tablespoons wine or malt vinegar
3 tablespoons water
1 tablespoon castor sugar
1 small onion, finely chopped
freshly ground pepper

Rice and pineapple salad

Serves 6
Cooking time 8 minutes

METRIC
225 g long-grain rice
1 (113-g) can pineapple rings
2 tablespoons seedless raisins or sultanas
Dressing
pinch of salt and pepper
½ teaspoon castor sugar
2 tablespoons vinegar
3 tablespoons oil
½ small onion, finely chopped
1 tablespoon finely chopped parsley

Add the rice to a pan of boiling salted water, re-boil and cook briskly for 8 minutes until rice grains are tender, then drain. Meanwhile drain the pineapple rings from the can and chop coarsely. Mix the cooked rice (while still warm) with the chopped pineapple and raisins or sultanas.

Blend together the seasonings, sugar and vinegar and add the oil, onion and parsley. Mix well and check the seasoning. Pour over rice mixture; toss well and leave until quite cold.
(*Illustrated on page 75*)

IMPERIAL
8 oz long-grain rice
1 (4-oz) can pineapple rings
2 tablespoons seedless raisins or sultanas
Dressing
pinch of salt and pepper
½ teaspoon castor sugar
2 tablespoons vinegar
3 tablespoons oil
½ small onion, finely chopped
1 tablespoon finely chopped parsley

Curried chicken salad

Serves 4

METRIC
4 cooked chicken joints
1 small head of celery
Dressing
150 ml mayonnaise
2 tablespoons single cream
salt and pepper
3 teaspoons curry paste
2 teaspoons lemon juice
1 teaspoon tomato purée

Take the meat from the cooked chicken joints and cut into dice. Separate the head of celery, trim and scrub clean then shred and add to the chicken. In a basin combine together the mayonnaise, single cream, a seasoning of salt and pepper, the curry paste, lemon juice and tomato purée. Add the dressing to the chicken flesh and toss to mix. Serve with a green salad.

IMPERIAL
4 cooked chicken joints
1 small head of celery
Dressing
¼ pint mayonnaise
2 tablespoons single cream
salt and pepper
3 teaspoons curry paste
2 teaspoons lemon juice
1 teaspoon tomato purée

Prawn salad

Serves 4

METRIC		IMPERIAL
450 g frozen prawns	Allow frozen prawns to thaw – discard excess juice which is inclined to make the dressing too thin. In a basin mix the prawns, mayonnaise, chopped shallot and parsley and add lemon juice to taste. One serving platter is really effective for this salad; arrange a few crisp lettuce leaves over the plate and pile the prawns on top. Sprinkle with a little extra chopped parsley and for a garnish arrange quartered hard-boiled eggs around the sides. Serve with a green salad and slices of brown bread and butter.	1 lb frozen prawns
2 tablespoons home-made mayonnaise		2 tablespoons home-made mayonnaise
1 teaspoon chopped shallot		1 teaspoon chopped shallot
1 tablespoon finely chopped parsley		1 tablespoon finely chopped parsley
squeeze of lemon juice		squeeze of lemon juice
Garnish		*Garnish*
crisp lettuce		crisp lettuce
2 hard-boiled eggs		2 hard-boiled eggs

(*Illustrated on page 58*)

Cottage cheese and fruit salad

Serves 4

METRIC		IMPERIAL
1 (227-g) carton cottage cheese	Spoon a little of the cottage cheese on to each of four drained pineapple slices. Serve with the washed leaves from the head of chicory and the sliced tomatoes.	1 (8-oz) carton cottage cheese
1 (227-g) can pineapple rings		1 (8-oz) can pineapple rings
1 head of chicory		1 head of chicory
4 medium-sized tomatoes		4 medium-sized tomatoes

Variations

Try any of the following combinations: thinly sliced peeled orange, cottage cheese and mustard and cress *or* peach halves, crisp lettuce heart, seedless raisins and cottage cheese *or* cottage cheese, grapefruit segments and endive *or* sliced tomatoes, seedless raisins and cottage cheese.

Salad dressings

Salad dressing can be made using oil and vinegar or lemon juice as a base with added flavouring, or a more creamy dressing can be made using mayonnaise, fresh or soured cream.

If salads are to be served frequently it's a good idea to make up a quantity of oil and vinegar dressing and store in the refrigerator in a screw-topped jar. Shake well before using.

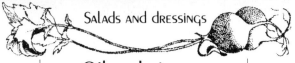
Oil and vinegar dressing

METRIC
salt and freshly ground pepper
½ teaspoon castor sugar
2 tablespoons wine vinegar
4 tablespoons olive oil

Put a generous seasoning of salt and pepper in a small mixing bowl. Add the sugar and vinegar and mix so that the vinegar dissolves all the seasonings. Add the oil and mix well. Taste to check the seasoning before serving.

If preferred lemon juice may be used instead of the vinegar. Use for tossing fresh lettuce, sliced tomatoes or cucumber, cold cooked new potatoes, carrots or asparagus tips.

IMPERIAL
salt and freshly ground pepper
½ teaspoon castor sugar
2 tablespoons wine vinegar
4 tablespoons olive oil

Variations

Fines herbes dressing Add 2 teaspoons chopped parsley or a mixture of parsley and chervil and a teaspoon chopped chives to the basic dressing. Serve with a green salad or vegetable salad.

Piquant dressing Add 1-2 teaspoons each finely chopped shallot, capers and gherkins to the basic dressing. Serve with potato salad.

Garlic dressing Add ½ clove of garlic, crushed, and 1 teaspoon chopped parsley to the basic dressing. Serve with chicory or endive.

Mint dressing Add 1 teaspoon finely chopped fresh mint to the basic dressing. Serve with potato salad, tomato salad, or a salad made with fresh pears.

Blue cheese dressing Add 25 g/1 oz crumbled Roquefort cheese to the basic dressing. Serve with a green salad to accompany a steak.

Tomato cream dressing Stir 1 tablespoon tomato ketchup and 2 tablespoons double cream into the basic dressing. Serve with fish salads or hard-boiled eggs.

Sour cream dressing

METRIC
1 (142-ml) carton soured cream
salt and freshly ground pepper
2-3 tablespoons oil and vinegar dressing (see page 72)
1 teaspoon chopped chives

Place the soured cream, seasonings, dressing and chopped chives in a small mixing bowl and blend thoroughly. Chill before serving.

Use for tossing cooked or canned flaked salmon or tuna fish or for new potato salad; this dressing is also delicious on a tomato salad.

IMPERIAL
1 (5-fl oz) carton soured cream
salt and freshly ground pepper
2-3 tablespoons oil and vinegar dressing (see page 72)
1 teaspoon chopped chives

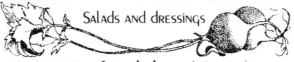
Seafood dressing

METRIC
2 tablespoons mayonnaise
2 tablespoons tomato ketchup
2 tablespoons double cream
dash of Tabasco sauce
1 teaspoon Worcestershire sauce
squeeze of lemon juice

Blend all the sauce ingredients together. Check the sharpness, adding more lemon juice if necessary. Use for tossing prepared prawns, lobster or crab flesh for cocktails. A nice addition is a little diced fresh melon.

IMPERIAL
2 tablespoons mayonnaise
2 tablespoons tomato ketchup
2 tablespoons double cream
dash of Tabasco sauce
1 teaspoon Worcestershire sauce
squeeze of lemon juice

Blender mayonnaise

METRIC
2 egg yolks
½ teaspoon salt
¼ teaspoon dry mustard
½ teaspoon pepper
2 teaspoons castor sugar
2 tablespoons vinegar
300 ml olive oil

Put the egg yolks, seasonings and sugar into a blender, and add 1 tablespoon of the vinegar. Using the lowest speed, just blend them together. Remove the centre cap in the blender top and begin pouring the oil very slowly on to the egg yolks, still on the lowest speed. Add the oil very gradually at first, almost drop by drop from the lip of the jug. The mayonnaise will not begin to thicken until the blades are about half covered by the mixture, but still continue adding the oil slowly. When beginning to thicken, continue adding the oil in a thin, steady stream, until only about a quarter of it is left. Then add the rest of the vinegar and the remaining oil.

Use the mayonnaise thinned down with a little cream if liked to toss cold cooked potato, quartered hard-boiled egg, cooked flaked fish or prepared shellfish.

IMPERIAL
2 egg yolks
½ teaspoon salt
¼ teaspoon dry mustard
½ teaspoon pepper
2 teaspoons castor sugar
2 tablespoons vinegar
½ pint olive oil

Spiced peaches to serve with cold meats

METRIC
1 (822-g) can peach halves
75 g soft brown sugar
4 tablespoons white malt vinegar
2·5-cm piece cinnamon stick
2 teaspoons whole cloves
2 teaspoons whole allspice

Drain the syrup from the can of peaches into a saucepan and stir in sugar, vinegar and spices. Bring slowly to the boil, stirring to dissolve the sugar, and simmer for 5 minutes. Add the peach halves, bring to the boil again and simmer for a further 5 minutes.

Draw the pan off the heat and put the peaches and spiced syrup into a dish; cool. Put in the refrigerator for a few hours, or overnight. Serve chilled with cold gammon or pork.

IMPERIAL
1 (1 lb 13-oz) can peach halves
3 oz soft brown sugar
4 tablespoons white malt vinegar
1-inch piece cinnamon stick
2 teaspoons whole cloves
2 teaspoons whole allspice

MINUTE SAVERS

If olive oil becomes solid in the bottle during cold weather, stand the bottle in a jug of warm water – the oil will quickly become liquid again.

Never toss green salad in oil and vinegar dressing until ready to serve; the acid in the vinegar makes the lettuce go limp.

Slice tomatoes with a serrated knife; it's often a good idea to use the bread knife – much quicker and easier for soft tomatoes.

If soured cream, mentioned in many of the recipes, is hard to buy use double cream sharpened with lemon juice.

After peeling or cutting onions, rinse your hands in cold water and rub with a little salt. If the smell still lingers, try rubbing with fresh parsley, crushing out the juice between your fingers, or with dry mustard, rinsing it off again under cold water.

Scalding tomatoes by covering them with boiling water and leaving them for about 10 seconds is the best method of peeling them. The minute skins begin to curl up, lift the tomatoes out with a perforated spoon and transfer at once to a bowl of cold water to cool quickly and keep the flesh firm. Peel off the skins. Use skinned tomatoes in salads and as a garnsh.

Meat sauce for pasta (see page 80)

Rice and pineapple salad (see page 70)

Speedy sauces

A basic white sauce is in itself quite simple and quick to make. For added speed and ease, either use a blending method where the milk and flour are whisked together before adding to the melted butter or make the roux mix of flour and butter beforehand and store ready for use.

All-in-one white sauce

Makes 300 ml/½ pint
Cooking time 2-3 minutes

METRIC		IMPERIAL
30 g butter or margarine		1 oz butter or margarine
300 ml milk		½ pint milk
30 g plain flour		1 oz plain flour
salt and pepper		salt and pepper

Place the butter or margarine in a saucepan and set over a low heat to melt. Meanwhile measure the cold milk into a medium-sized mixing bowl and sift the flour on to it. Using a whisk or rotary hand beater, mix the two quickly and thoroughly together.

Pour the blended milk into the melted fat and cook, stirring all the time, until the mixture has thickened and is boiling. Cook the mixture for 2-3 minutes, then season well with salt and pepper and use as required.

This method makes a medium thick pouring sauce; if a thinner sauce is required, add a little extra milk. For a thicker sauce, use a little less milk than the recipe states. Always remember it is easier to add extra milk afterwards.

Variations

There are many variations to any basic sauce; always remember to cook the sauce and season to taste before adding any of the extra ingredients.

Cheese sauce Add 50 g/2 oz grated Cheddar cheese and ¼ teaspoon made mustard, after the sauce has cooked. Stir until cheese has melted. Serve over fish, eggs, macaroni or vegetables.

Note If the sauce is to be used as a base for macaroni and cheese, increase the cheese in the sauce to 75 g/3 oz.

Caper sauce Add about 2 teaspoons of chopped capers and a squeeze of lemon juice to the sauce after it has cooked. Serve over boiled mutton or veal.

Shrimp sauce Add a few picked shrimps or a small carton of potted shrimps to the cooked sauce. Add a little anchovy essence for extra flavour or a tablespoon tomato ketchup if a pink sauce is required. Serve over fish dishes.

BleNder hollaNdaise sauce

Serves 4

METRIC
2 egg yolks
1 tablespoon lemon juice
pinch of salt and pepper
100g butter or margarine

Place the egg yolks in a blender together with the lemon juice and seasoning. Cover and quickly blend. Heat the butter until melted and almost boiling then draw off the heat. Turn the blender on at high speed, and slowly pour the butter on to the egg mixture. Blend well until thick and fluffy; about 30 seconds. Stand the sauce over warm water until ready to be used.

Serve over cooked broccoli or asparagus.

IMPERIAL
2 egg yolks
1 tablespoon lemon juice
pinch of salt and pepper
4 oz butter or margarine

CaNNed tomato sauce

Serves 4
Cooking time 5 minutes

METRIC
1 onion, peeled and finely chopped
15 g butter
1 (425-g) can tomatoes
water (see method)
2 tablespoons cornflour
1 tablespoon castor sugar
½ teaspoon dried mixed herbs
salt and freshly ground pepper

Add the onion to the melted butter in a saucepan. Cook gently for 2-3 minutes to soften the onion but do not allow to brown. Add the contents of the can of tomatoes and half the can of water blended with the cornflour, sugar (tomatoes always taste better with a little sweetness), herbs and a seasoning of salt and pepper. Stir until the mixture is boiling and thickened, then simmer gently for 5 minutes. Draw the pan off the heat, and pass the sauce through a sieve. Check the seasoning and serve.

IMPERIAL
1 onion, peeled and finely chopped
½ oz butter
1 (15-oz) can tomatoes
water (see method)
2 tablespoons cornflour
1 tablespoon castor sugar
½ teaspoon dried mixed herbs
salt and freshly ground pepper

Quick barbecue sauce

Serves 4
Cooking time 5 minutes

METRIC
2 tablespoons salad oil
1 onion, finely chopped
200 ml tomato ketchup
4 tablespoons vinegar
50 g soft brown sugar
2 teaspoons made mustard
2 tablespoons Worcestershire sauce
½ teaspoon salt

Heat the oil in a small saucepan, add the onion and fry gently for 5 minutes until tender. Add all the remaining ingredients; bring slowly to the boil and allow to simmer for 5 minutes.

Use as a baste for kebabs, grilled sausages or hamburgers.

IMPERIAL
2 tablespoons salad oil
1 onion, finely chopped
⅓ pint tomato ketchup
4 tablespoons vinegar
2 oz soft brown sugar
2 teaspoons made mustard
2 tablespoons Worcestershire sauce
½ teaspoon salt

Fresh mushroom sauce

Serves 4
Cooking time 1-2 minutes

METRIC		IMPERIAL
25 g butter		1 oz butter
100 g button mushrooms		4 oz button mushrooms
salt and pepper		salt and pepper
pinch of dried mixed herbs		pinch of dried mixed herbs
1 tablespoon flour		1 tablespoon flour
150 ml creamy milk		$\frac{1}{4}$ pint creamy milk
1 tablespoon chopped parsley		1 tablespoon chopped parsley

Melt the butter in a frying pan over a moderate heat and add the prepared mushrooms. Button mushrooms are the small closed mushrooms; they are the best kind to use in a sauce because they look nicer and they do not discolour the sauce as much as the very black open ones. Cultivated mushrooms do not need peeling; rinse under cold water, trim stalks, pat dry and slice.

Fry the mushrooms fairly quickly for about 1 minute, tossing them to cook evenly. Add a good seasoning of salt and freshly ground pepper, herbs and the flour. Stir to blend and then gradually stir in the milk and bring up to the boil, stirring all the time until thickened. Allow to simmer gently for 1-2 minutes, add parsley and draw off heat. If overcooked, mushroom sauce will discolour very quickly due to the dark juices being drawn out of the mushrooms.

Serve with steak, liver, chicken or kidneys.

Meat sauce for pasta

Makes 600 ml/1 pint
Cooking time about 45 minutes

METRIC		IMPERIAL
2 tablespoons oil		2 tablespoons oil
1 medium-sized onion		1 medium-sized onion
1 clove of garlic		1 clove of garlic
450 g lean minced beef		1 lb lean minced beef
1 teaspoon salt		1 teaspoon salt
freshly ground pepper		freshly ground pepper
1 (425-g) can peeled tomatoes		1 (15-oz) can peeled tomatoes
1 (64-g) can tomato purée		1 (2$\frac{1}{4}$-oz) can tomato purée
pinch of dried mixed herbs		pinch of dried mixed herbs
150 ml stock		$\frac{1}{4}$ pint stock
150 ml red wine		$\frac{1}{4}$ pint red wine
Garnish		*Garnish*
little chopped parsley		little chopped parsley

Heat the oil in a medium-sized saucepan. Peel and finely chop the onion, peel the garlic and crush to a purée with a little salt. Add the onion to the hot oil, cover and cook gently for about 5 minutes until the onion is soft but not brown. Stir in the minced beef. Stir to brown on all sides.

Stir the salt, pepper, tomatoes, tomato purée and mixed herbs into the meat mixture. Add the stock and red wine. Bring to the boil. Lower the heat and simmer gently for 40-45 minutes. Stir occasionally to prevent the sauce sticking and add a little extra stock if necessary. The final consistency should not be too thick. Check the seasoning and use as required.

(*Illustrated on page 76*)

80

Devil sauce

Serves 4
Cooking time 5 minutes

Add the onion to the melted butter and cook gently over a low heat for about 5 minutes to soften the onion. Add the Worcestershire sauce, mushroom ketchup, tomatoes, stock and a seasoning of salt and pepper. Bring slowly up to the boil, stirring occasionally. Cream together the butter and flour and stir into the sauce to thicken. Simmer for 5 minutes.
Serve with steak, chops or fried chicken joints.

METRIC	IMPERIAL
1 large onion, peeled and finely chopped or minced	1 large onion, peeled and finely chopped or minced
15 g butter, melted	$\frac{1}{2}$ oz butter, melted
3 tablespoons Worcestershire sauce	3 tablespoons Worcestershire sauce
1 tablespoon mushroom ketchup	1 tablespoon mushroom ketchup
1 (227-g) can tomatoes	1 (8-oz) can tomatoes
150 ml stock or water plus stock cube	$\frac{1}{4}$ pint stock or water plus stock cube
salt and pepper	salt and pepper
15 g butter	$\frac{1}{2}$ oz butter
1 tablespoon flour	1 tablespoon flour

Pineapple
sweet and sour sauce

Serves 4-6
Cooking time 5 minutes

Drain the pineapple from the can and reserve the syrup, making it up to 300 ml/ $\frac{1}{2}$ pint with water. Combine this with the vinegar, brown sugar, soy sauce and salt. Measure the cornflour into a medium-sized saucepan and moisten with a little of the liquid, mixing to a smooth paste. Stir in the remaining liquid and cook over moderate heat until thickened and boiling. Add pineapple chunks and draw pan off the heat.
Serve with pork chops or grilled gammon rashers.

METRIC	IMPERIAL
1 (339-g) can pineapple chunks	1 (12-oz) can pineapple chunks
4 tablespoons vinegar	4 tablespoons vinegar
75 g soft brown sugar	3 oz soft brown sugar
1 tablespoon soy sauce	1 tablespoon soy sauce
$\frac{1}{4}$ teaspoon salt	$\frac{1}{4}$ teaspoon salt
2 tablespoons cornflour	2 tablespoons cornflour

Quick sauces
using a ready-made roux

If you're a cook who uses sauces a good deal it might be an advantage to make the roux, that is the cooked butter and flour basis for any sauce, in a quantity and store it in the refrigerator ready made. This is particularly time saving for brown sauces where the roux may take up to 40 minutes to colour properly.

It's best to make one mix to be used for white sauce — it's important that this roux does not brown, otherwise the resulting sauce would be discoloured — and a second mix for brown sauce — this roux in fact has to be cooked until quite dark in colour.

To make a roux mix for white sauces Melt 225 g/8 oz butter or margarine in a heavy saucepan and stir in 225 g/8 oz plain flour. Cook over low heat, stirring occasionally to prevent the mix from sticking to the pan base and browning. As the roux cooks it will become lighter in colour and slightly sandy or crumbly in texture. When ready – it takes about 15 minutes – draw the pan off the heat and allow to stand until cool, stirring occasionally. Then spoon into a screw-topped jar; cover and store in the refrigerator.

To use the roux for white sauces Heat 300 ml/$\frac{1}{2}$ pint milk in a saucepan until almost boiling. Then draw the pan off the heat and add 2 tablespoons of the roux mix. Stir until the roux has melted then replace over a moderate heat and stir until the sauce thickens and is boiling. Cook gently for 2-3 minutes then season well and use as required. Any of the variations given for basic white sauce may be used with this sauce.

To make a roux mix for brown sauces Melt 225 g/8 oz white cooking fat or dripping in a heavy saucepan and stir in 350 g/12 oz plain flour. This time cook gently, stirring occasionally but allow the roux to brown gently and evenly. Eventually the mixture should be quite dark brown in colour, but take care not to allow it to burn. When ready – it takes about 40 minutes – draw the pan off the heat and allow to cool, stirring occasionally. Then spoon into a screw-topped jar; cover and store in the refrigerator.

To use the roux for brown sauces Heat 450 ml/$\frac{3}{4}$ pint water in a saucepan until almost boiling, then crumble in a beef or chicken stock cube and stir until dissolved. Draw the pan off the heat and add 3 tablespoons of brown roux mix. Stir until the roux has melted, then replace the pan over a moderate heat and stir until the sauce has thickened and boiled. Cook for 2-3 minutes then season well with salt and pepper and use as required.

Variations of the basic brown sauce

Espagnole sauce Follow the recipe above, using only 300 ml/$\frac{1}{2}$ pint water and a 425-g/15-oz can tomatoes. Add a few bacon rinds and chopped mushrooms for flavour and simmer for an extra 10 minutes. Strain the sauce before using.

Use the sauce in basic stews or casseroles, or serve with fried liver or meat or for re-heating cold slices of beef or lamb.

Piquante sauce Into the basic brown sauce, stir 1 teaspoon made mustard, 1 tablespoon red-currant jelly, $\frac{1}{2}$ teaspoon paprika (not the hot cayenne pepper) and 1 tablespoon vinegar. Simmer to dissolve the jelly and blend flavourings.

Serve with sausages and hamburgers.

Curry sauce Prepare the basic brown sauce and, while simmering, in a separate saucepan melt 15 g/$\frac{1}{2}$ oz butter; add a peeled and finely chopped onion. Cover with a lid and fry gently to soften the onion, stir in 2 tablespoons curry powder, or more for a hot curry, and fry gently for a further 5 minutes. Then stir in the cooked brown sauce, 1 tablespoon sweet chutney – chop up any large pieces – and a squeeze of lemon juice. Bring up to the boil and serve.

Excellent with cooked meat or quartered hard-boiled eggs. Or pour over fresh cubed steak or chicken joints and casserole in the oven following a normal curry recipe.

Mushroom sauce Prepare the basic brown sauce and, while simmering, in a separate pan fry 100 g/4 oz trimmed sliced mushrooms in 25 g/1 oz butter. Stir in the cooked sauce, re-heat and serve with sausages, hamburgers, liver or steak.

CREAM SAUCES FOR MEAT, fish, poulTRy ANd VEGETAblES

A number of quick sauces can be made using fresh or soured cream as a basis. Extra flavourings come from ketchups, table sauces, herbs, seasonings and spices.

Speedy SAUCES

PARSLEY CREAM SAUCE

Serves 4

METRIC
150 ml double or soured cream
squeeze of lemon juice
salt and freshly ground pepper
1 teaspoon finely chopped parsley or chives

After fresh or frozen vegetables are cooked and drained, return them to the hot pan, add the cream and lemon juice to sharpen the flavour and a seasoning of salt and pepper. Add the parsley or chives and toss to mix. Allow to warm through but only gently; do not boil.

IMPERIAL
¼ pint double or soured cream
squeeze of lemon juice
salt and freshly ground pepper
1 teaspoon finely chopped parsley or chives

SOUR CREAM HORSERADISH SAUCE

Serves 4-6

METRIC
4 tablespoons prepared horseradish relish
1 (142-ml) carton soured cream
salt and freshly ground pepper
dash of Worcestershire sauce

In a basin mix together the horseradish relish and soured cream. Add a seasoning of salt and pepper and a dash of Worcestershire sauce. Allow to stand for 1 hour before serving.
Serve with hot or cold roast beef, and grilled steaks.

IMPERIAL
4 tablespoons prepared horseradish relish
1 (5-fl oz) carton soured cream
salt and freshly ground pepper
dash of Worcestershire sauce

AVOCADO SAUCE

Serves 4

METRIC
1 ripe avocado pear
4-6 tablespoons oil and vinegar dressing (see page 72)
1 (142-ml) carton soured cream

Halve the avocado pear, remove the stone and scoop out the flesh into a basin. Using a fork, mash until smooth, then stir in the French dressing, soured cream and a seasoning of salt and pepper. Taste and serve with any cold meat or ham, or cold poached fish such as salmon or trout.

IMPERIAL
1 ripe avocado pear
4-6 tablespoons oil and vinegar dressing (see page 72)
1 (5-fl oz) carton soured cream

MUSTARD CREAM SAUCE

Serves 4

METRIC
150 ml double cream
1 tablespoon prepared English mustard
salt and pepper

Lightly whip the cream. Fold in the mustard and a seasoning of salt and pepper to taste.
Serve with herrings, mackerel or grilled fish.

IMPERIAL
¼ pint double cream
1 tablespoon prepared English mustard
salt and pepper

83

Stroganoff sauce

Serves 2-3

METRIC		IMPERIAL
1 small onion	Peel and finely chop the onion. Melt the	1 small onion
25 g butter	butter in a frying pan, add the onion and	1 oz butter
50 g button mushrooms	fry gently for a few minutes to soften.	2 oz button mushrooms
½ teaspoon tomato purée	Trim and slice the mushrooms, add to the	½ teaspoon tomato purée
1 (142-ml) carton soured cream	pan and cook gently for about 5 minutes. Stir in the tomato purée and soured	1 (5-fl oz) carton soured cream
salt and freshly ground pepper	cream and bring just up to the boil. Season to taste with salt and pepper and serve hot with grilled steak or chicken.	salt and freshly ground pepper

Cucumber sauce

Serves 4

METRIC		IMPERIAL
½ cucumber	Peel and halve the cucumber lengthwise.	½ cucumber
1 (142-ml) carton soured cream	Remove the centre seeds and finely chop the flesh. Add to the soured cream along	1 (5-fl oz) carton soured cream
salt and pepper	with a seasoning of salt and pepper, and	salt and pepper
squeeze of lemon juice	the lemon juice to sharpen the flavour.	squeeze of lemon juice
1 teaspoon finely grated onion	Stir in the onion and chopped parsley. Serve with hot or cold salmon or grilled	1 teaspoon finely grated onion
1 teaspoon chopped parsley	mackerel.	1 teaspoon chopped parsley

Minute savers

When making a traditional white sauce — warm the milk to be added to the roux of butter and flour, it blends in much more quickly and evenly.

To keep a ready-made sauce warm for some time, cover the surface of the sauce with a square of wetted greaseproof paper close to the surface with the wet side downwards. Stand the base of the pan in a shallow tin of simmering water — this prevents scorching.

To make a brown roux quickly — brown the flour on a baking tray in the oven before making the sauce.

Keep a jar of seasoned flour handy for making sauces. For every 25 g/1 oz flour sift with 1 teaspoon salt and ½ teaspoon pepper.

A blend of butter and flour called beurre manié is often used to thicken sauces, soups or casseroles at the end of the cooking time. Work 40 g/1½ oz butter with 25 g/1 oz flour on a plate with a knife until it forms a paste. Add in small pieces to the pan off the heat. The butter melts and draws the flour into the liquid. Return to the heat and stir until thickened. This has many useful applications, particularly for mixtures that have not thickened adequately

You can keep a white sauce hot without a skin forming on the surface if you stir in all but about 2-3 tablespoons of the milk for mixing during preparation. Bring the sauce to the boil, season and simmer for a few minutes to cook. Then turn heat to very low and add the reserved milk so that it lies on the surface. Do not stir until just before serving.

GUEST APPEARANCES

In the corner of a store cupboard always keep special items for occasions when friends drop in unexpectedly. Cans of soup or consommé, salted nuts, jars of olives, small cans of pâté, sardines or anchovies all keep well. Quick dips or savouries can be made to serve with drinks. If guests stay, a simple starter is easy enough to make and can be followed by a snack meal with cheese and biscuits for dessert.

Appetisers

Marinated olives

Serves 4

METRIC
1 (148-g) jar green olives
pinch of salt, pepper and dry mustard
pinch of sugar
1 tablespoon white vinegar
3 tablespoons vegetable oil
1 tablespoon water
1 small clove of garlic, peeled and quartered

Drain the liquid from the jar of olives, then tip them into a small bowl and set the jar aside.

Into this jar measure the seasonings and vinegar, shaking slightly to blend; then add the oil and water and screw on the lid, shaking vigorously to blend. Remove the lid, add the olives along with the garlic and screw the lid on again. Shake once or twice to coat the olives with the dressing, then store in a cool place overnight to marinate, but not in the refrigerator.
(*Illustrated on page 93*)

IMPERIAL
1 (5½-oz) jar green olives
pinch of salt, pepper and dry mustard
pinch of sugar
1 tablespoon white vinegar
3 tablespoons vegetable oil
1 tablespoon water
1 small clove of garlic, peeled and quartered

Quick cheese straws

Makes about 36
Cooking time 8-10 minutes

METRIC
225 g ready-made puff pastry
made mustard
pepper
50-75 g cheese, grated

On a lightly floured working surface roll out the pastry thinly. Spread one half with ready-made mustard — it's best to use English mustard — and a little freshly ground pepper. Sprinkle with grated cheese and then fold the other half over.

Roll out to make a little thinner, then using a sharp knife cut first into 5-cm/2-inch wide strips of pastry, then into thin fingers. Arrange on a wetted baking tray and cook in a hot oven (220°C, 425°F, Gas Mark 7) for 8-10 minutes, until golden brown and crisp.
(*Illustrated on page 93*)

IMPERIAL
8 oz ready-made puff pastry
made mustard
pepper
2-3 oz cheese, grated

Party dip

METRIC
2 tablespoons oil and vinegar dressing (see page 72)
225 g cream cheese
2 tablespoons tomato ketchup
½ small onion, finely chopped
1 teaspoon anchovy essence

Gradually beat the dressing into the cream cheese and blend thoroughly. Add the remaining ingredients and mix well. Set aside until ready to serve.

Serve the dip with a selection of raw prepared vegetables such as cauliflower florets, carrot strips, celery, mushrooms, cucumber strips and cabbage slices.

IMPERIAL
2 tablespoons oil and vinegar dressing (see page 72)
8 oz cream cheese
2 tablespoons tomato ketchup
½ small onion, finely chopped
1 teaspoon anchovy essence

Herring roe savouries

Makes about 32
Cooking time 5 minutes

METRIC
1 (106-g) can cooked herring roes
50 g butter
1 teaspoon made mustard
2 teaspoons Worcestershire sauce
salt and pepper
lemon juice
8 small slices white bread, toasted
1 (56-g) can anchovies

Drain the herring roes from the can and cream with the butter, mustard and Worcestershire sauce. Season with salt and pepper and add a squeeze of lemon juice. Then spread on toasted slices of bread. Top with anchovy slices and grill until hot. Quickly trim away crusts, cut into fingers and serve hot.

IMPERIAL
1 (3½-oz) can cooked herring roes
2 oz butter
1 teaspoon made mustard
2 teaspoons Worcestershire sauce
salt and pepper
lemon juice
8 small slices white bread, toasted
1 (2-oz) can anchovies

Parmesan toasties Brush small savoury crackers with melted butter, sprinkle with garlic salt and then grated Parmesan cheese. Cook in a moderate oven (180°C, 350°F, Gas Mark 4) until hot and golden.

Potato chip canapés Soften liver sausage or canned pâté with a little cream or mayonnaise and drop by spoonfuls on to crisp potato chips.

Hot potato chips Heat the oven to moderate (180°C, 350°F, Gas Mark 4). Spread 1 packet plain potato chips on a baking tray and dust generously with garlic or onion salt. Heat through in the oven for 5 minutes and serve warm.

Cream cheese and anchovy toast Cut slices of toast into 5-cm/2-in squares. Spread thinly with anchovy paste. Soften cream cheese with a little milk and, using a piping tube, make a border of cream cheese round each square.

Cheese sticks Take pieces of sharp Cheddar or milder Gouda and cut into cubes. Top some with small stuffed olives, some with small pickled onions, others with maraschino cherries. Spear both together with a toothpick and arrange on a dish (*Illustrated on page 93*)

Salty radishes Wash radishes and trim away the large green leaves, leaving a few of the more tender green leaves on. Serve with salt for dipping into. (*Illustrated on page 93*)

Melon balls with ham Take a ripe cantaloupe or honeydew melon and make it into balls with a melon baller. Take paper thin slices of Parma ham, and cut them into thin strips. Wrap one strip around each melon ball. Spear with a toothpick to serve.

Garlic olives Place 1 peeled clove of garlic in a bowl. Add a tablespoon each of olive oil and drained green olives. Toss together and chill for several hours before serving. For a stronger flavour, chop the garlic clove first.

EASY STARTERS

TOMATOES STUFFED WITH CREAM CHEESE

Serves 4

METRIC
8 ripe medium-sized tomatoes
175-225 g cream cheese
squeeze of lemon juice

Scald the tomatoes and peel away the skins. Cut a slice off the top of each and using a teaspoon scoop out the seeds. Sprinkle with salt and turn the tomato cups upside down to drain.

Using a wooden spoon, blend together the cream cheese and lemon juice. Pile the cheese mixture into the tomato cups and replace the lids. Serve with thinly sliced brown bread and butter.

IMPERIAL
8 ripe medium-sized tomatoes
6-8 oz cream cheese
squeeze of lemon juice

SARDINE-STUFFED EGGS

Serves 4
Cooking time 6 minutes

METRIC
4 eggs
1 (120-g) can sardines
salt and pepper
squeeze of lemon juice
1 tablespoon cream, mayonnaise or top of the milk
8 buttered brown bread slices

Hard-boil the eggs, remove the shells and slice the eggs in half lengthwise. With the tip of a knife blade push the yolks out of the whites into a mixing bowl. Add the sardines, bones and tails removed, and mash the ingredients with a fork. Season with salt and pepper to taste and beat in the lemon juice and cream, mayonnaise or milk.

Cut thin slices off the base of each white half egg to make them steady and arrange on the buttered brown bread slices. (Reserve the pieces of egg white for garnish.) Spoon or pipe the filling back into the halves, dividing it equally between each one. Top with slices of egg white, and serve with extra brown bread and butter.

IMPERIAL
4 eggs
1 (4¼-oz) can sardines
salt and pepper
squeeze of lemon juice
1 tablespoon cream, mayonnaise or top of the milk
8 buttered brown bread slices

GRAPEFRUIT COCKTAIL

Serves 4

METRIC
1 (567-g) can grapefruit segments
1 tablespoon crème de menthe

Empty the grapefruit segments and juice into a mixing bowl. Add the crème de menthe and stir to blend the flavour and colour. When ready to serve, divide the segments between four cocktail glasses and spoon over the juice.

IMPERIAL
1 (1¼-lb) can grapefruit segments
1 tablespoon crème de menthe

Soufflé au parfait

Serves 4
Cooking time 40-50 minutes

METRIC		IMPERIAL
50 g butter	Melt the butter in a medium to large saucepan over a low heat. Stir in the flour and cook gently for 1 minute. Gradually beat in the milk stirring all the time to make a thick sauce. Bring up to the boil then draw the pan off the heat, add a generous seasoning of salt and pepper and a pinch of nutmeg. Remove the pâté from the cans and cut into chunks, add to the sauce and stir until melted and blended into the mixture.	2 oz butter
50 g plain flour		2 oz plain flour
300 ml milk		$\frac{1}{2}$ pint milk
salt and pepper		salt and pepper
pinch of nutmeg		pinch of nutmeg
2 (113-g) cans Swiss pâté		2 (4-oz) cans Swiss pâté
4 eggs		4 eggs

Separate the eggs and beat the egg yolks into the pâté mixture. Whisk the whites in a mixing bowl until stiff and, using a metal spoon, fold into the mixture. Pour into a buttered 18-cm/7-inch soufflé or round baking dish and cook in a moderate oven (180°C, 350°F, Gas Mark 4) for 40-50 minutes. Serve at once with a tossed salad.

Quick soups

To make any soup your own speciality in an instant, dress it up with a garnish or serve with hot breads. Soups lend themselves to a variety of garnishes — anything from a sprinkling of chopped parsley to grated cheese. Parmesan croûtons are a delicious accompaniment.

Sprinkle crumbled fried bacon pieces, grated cheese, paprika pepper, chopped parsley or toast slices cut in tiny dice, over tomato, asparagus, celery, mushroom or any vegetable soup.

Stir chopped chives, fresh cream, diced hard-boiled eggs, chopped green pepper or snipped watercress leaves into any cream soup. Chives are specially tasty in potato soup.

Cut thin slices of lemon or cucumber and float on top of consommé, beef or chicken bouillon or oxtail soup.

Add sliced frankfurter sausages or grated cheese to heartier soups such as Scotch broth, lentil, vegetable or chicken and rice.

Parmesan croûtons

Serves 4
Cooking time few minutes

METRIC		IMPERIAL
3 slices white bread, crusts removed	Cut the bread into 5-mm/$\frac{1}{4}$-inch cubes and sauté in the hot butter or margarine until golden brown. Add the cheese, tossing to mix well then serve hot.	3 slices white bread, crusts removed
25 g butter or margarine		1 oz butter or margarine
2 tablespoons grated Parmesan cheese		2 tablespoons grated Parmesan cheese

Melba toast

Serves 4

METRIC		IMPERIAL
6 slices white bread, crusts removed	First toast the bread slices on both sides until golden brown. Carefully split each one into two thin slices. Cut each new slice diagonally to make triangles and toast again, the insides this time. Cool and store in an airtight tin.	6 slices white bread, crusts removed

Canned and packet soups

Canned soups have tremendous advantages for a busy cook and since they store well, it is a good plan to have a wide selection always in stock. Soups of different flavours can be combined together or, to basic cream or condensed soups, extra vegetables may be added. For instance a small can of creamed-style sweetcorn may be stirred into tomato soup; a can of drained, cut asparagus spears make cream or condensed asparagus look like home-made; to chicken soup add thawed frozen peas; or heat up beef consommé with a tablespoon of sherry and serve with a garnish of thinly sliced lemon or chopped parsley.

In summer or for any special occasion, fresh iced soups make a pleasant change. Serve them really cold in chilled soup bowls. For simple quick recipes, cream of asparagus, celery, chicken, mushroom or tomato soup all made with milk and chilled are delicious. Beef consommé can be chilled in the can or poured into a bowl with 1 tablespoon of sherry added before serving. Serve any of the soups topped with chopped parsley or chives.

For quantities, remember a 298-g/$10\frac{1}{2}$-oz can of cream soup will serve two and a 298-g/$10\frac{1}{2}$-oz can of condensed soup will give three to four servings. When preparing condensed soups, empty the soup into a saucepan and stir to make it smooth. Then gradually add the water or milk, stirring it in a little at a time.

Packet soups, which take anything from five to thirty minutes to prepare, are also worth keeping on hand.

Hearty broth

Serves 4
Cooking time 5 minutes

METRIC		IMPERIAL
2-3 rashers back bacon	Trim the bacon rashers and chop coarsely. Fry gently in a saucepan until the fat runs, then stir in the contents of both cans of soup. Gradually stir in the water and bring slowly up to the boil. Drain the cocktail sausages or frankfurters from the can; slice the frankfurters thickly. Add to the soup along with the frozen peas and stir until almost boiling, then simmer gently for 5 minutes. Serve with buttered whole-meal rolls.	2-3 rashers back bacon
1 (298-g) can condensed pea soup		1 (10½-oz) can condensed pea soup
1 (298-g) can condensed vegetable soup		1 (10½-oz) can condensed vegetable soup
2 soup cans water		2 soup cans water
1 (170-g) can cocktail sausages or 1 (114-g) can frankfurter sausages		1 (6-oz) can cocktail sausages or 1 (4-oz) can frankfurter sausages
1 (114-g) packet frozen peas with mint		1 (4-oz) packet frozen peas with mint

COUNTRY VEGETABLE SOUP

Serves 6
Cooking time 15 minutes

Trim the bacon rashers and chop finely. Fry very gently in a saucepan until the fat runs, then add the onion and fry a further few minutes to soften the onion. Add the contents of the two cans of soup and stir to blend, then gradually stir in the water. Heat gently almost to boiling point, then draw the pan off the heat. Serve at once.

METRIC
2-3 rashers lean bacon
1 medium onion, finely chopped or grated
1 (298-g) can condensed cream of mushroom soup
1 (298-g) can condensed vegetable soup
2 soup cans water

IMPERIAL
2-3 rashers lean bacon
1 medium onion, finely chopped or grated
1 ($10\frac{1}{2}$-oz) can condensed cream of mushroom soup
1 ($10\frac{1}{2}$-oz) can condensed vegetable soup
2 soup cans water

TOMATO VEGETABLE SOUP

Serves 4-6
Cooking time few minutes

Blend the soups together in a saucepan and gradually stir in the water. Heat stirring occasionally until almost boiling, then draw off the heat. Serve sprinkled with cheese.

METRIC
1 (298-g) can condensed vegetable soup
1 (298-g) can condensed tomato soup
2 soup cans water
Garnish
grated cheese

IMPERIAL
1 ($10\frac{1}{2}$-oz) can condensed vegetable soup
1 ($10\frac{1}{2}$-oz) can condensed tomato soup
2 soup cans water
Garnish
grated cheese

TOMATO AND CELERY SOUP

Serves 6
Cooking time few minutes

Empty the contents of both cans into a saucepan and stir to blend. Gradually stir in the milk or stock and bring almost to the boil. Draw the pan off the heat, stir in the parsley and serve.

METRIC
1 (298-g) can condensed tomato soup
1 (298-g) can condensed celery soup
2 soup cans milk or stock or mixture of both
1 tablespoon finely chopped parsley

IMPERIAL
1 ($10\frac{1}{2}$-oz) can condensed tomato soup
1 ($10\frac{1}{2}$-oz) can condensed celery soup
2 soup cans milk or stock or mixture of both
1 tablespoon finely chopped parsley

CREAM OF CHICKEN SOUP

Serves 4-5
Cooking time few minutes

Empty the soup into a saucepan and stir in the stock. Add a pinch of dried thyme and bring almost to the boil. Stir in the cream, check the seasoning and serve.

METRIC
1 (298-g) can condensed cream of chicken soup
450 ml water plus chicken stock cube
pinch of dried thyme
150 ml single cream
salt and pepper

IMPERIAL
1 ($10\frac{1}{2}$-oz) can condensed cream of chicken soup
$\frac{3}{4}$ pint water plus chicken stock cube
pinch of dried thyme
$\frac{1}{4}$ pint single cream
salt and pepper

Mushroom and
sweetcorn soup

Serves 4
Cooking time 10 minutes

Marinated olives (see page 86); Salty radishes (see page 87); Quick cheese straws (see page 86); Cheese sticks (see page 87)

METRIC		IMPERIAL
25 g butter	Heat the butter in a saucepan, add the onion and fry gently for 5 minutes to soften. Draw the pan off the heat and stir in the sweetcorn and condensed mushroom soup. Gradually stir in the milk or water, replace over the heat and stir until almost boiling. Serve at once.	1 oz butter
1 onion, finely sliced		1 onion, finely sliced
1 (198-g) can cream-style sweetcorn		1 (7-oz) can cream-style sweetcorn
1 (298-g) can condensed mushroom soup		1 (10½-oz) can condensed mushroom soup
1 soup can milk or water		1 soup can milk or water

Tomato crab bisque

Serves 4
Cooking time few minutes

METRIC		IMPERIAL
1 (298-g) can condensed cream of tomato soup	Empty the contents of the soup can into a saucepan and gradually stir in the milk. Flake the crab flesh, discarding any sinews and add to the soup along with the lemon juice or sherry and cooked rice or peas. Heat gently until almost boiling. Serve with thin slices of brown bread and butter.	1 (10½-oz) can condensed cream of tomato soup
1 soup can milk		1 soup can milk
1 (198-g) can crab meat		1 (7-oz) can crab meat
dash of lemon juice or		dash of lemon juice or
1 tablespoon dry sherry		1 tablespoon dry sherry
1-2 tablespoons cooked rice or peas		1-2 tablespoons cooked rice or peas

Chilled summer soup

Serves 9

METRIC		IMPERIAL
2 (298-g) cans condensed tomato soup	Combine the soup, water and soured cream. Beat with a rotary beater until smooth then chill for several hours. Serve in chilled soup bowls, sprinkled with parsley or chives.	2 (10½-oz) cans condensed tomato soup
1½ soup cans water		1½ soup cans water
1 (142-ml) carton soured cream		1 (5-fl oz) carton soured cream
Garnish		*Garnish*
chopped parsley or chives		chopped parsley or chives

Curried chicken soup

Serves 4

METRIC		IMPERIAL
1 (298-g) can condensed cream of chicken soup	Pour the soup, milk and curry powder into a mixing bowl and blend until smooth. Chill in a refrigerator until ready to serve. Pour into chilled soup bowls and sprinkle the tops with parsley.	1 (10½-oz) can condensed cream of chicken soup
1 soup can milk		1 soup can milk
½ teaspoon curry powder		½ teaspoon curry powder
Garnish		*Garnish*
2 tablespoons chopped parsley		2 tablespoons chopped parsley

Chicken soup bowl

Serves 4
Cooking time 10 minutes

METRIC
1 small onion, peeled and chopped
15 g butter
1 (298-g) can condensed cream of chicken soup
1 soup can mixed milk and water
1 (312-g) can cream-style sweetcorn
2 3 tablespoons diced cooked chicken (or buy a cooked chicken joint and dice the flesh)

Add the chopped onion to the hot butter in a saucepan, cover with a lid and fry very gently until the onion is soft. This takes about 5 minutes – take care not to allow the onion to brown. Stir in the chicken soup and the mixed milk and water. Add the sweetcorn and cooked chicken flesh and continue to heat gently until hot but do not allow to boil. Serve with soft buttered rolls.

IMPERIAL
1 small onion, peeled and chopped
½ oz butter
1 (10½-oz) can condensed cream of chicken soup
1 soup can mixed milk and water
1 (11-oz) can cream-style sweetcorn
2-3 tablespoons diced cooked chicken (or buy a cooked chicken joint and dice the flesh)

Celery and cheese soup bowl

Serves 4-6
Cooking time 5 minutes

METRIC
1 (298-g) can condensed cream of celery soup
1½ soup cans milk
100 g Cheddar cheese, grated
¼ teaspoon Worcestershire sauce
½ teaspoon salt
pinch of pepper
Garnish
chopped parsley

Empty the contents of the soup can into a saucepan and gradually stir in the milk. Add the cheese, Worcestershire sauce, salt and pepper. Stir over a moderate heat until the cheese melts and soup is hot but do not allow to boil. Draw off the heat; sprinkle with parsley. Serve with fresh croissants and butter.

IMPERIAL
1 (10½-oz) can condensed cream of celery soup
1½ soup cans milk
4 oz Cheddar cheese, grated
¼ teaspoon Worcestershire sauce
½ teaspoon salt
pinch of pepper
Garnish
chopped parsley

Bean chowder

Serves 4-6
Cooking time few minutes

METRIC
1 (298-g) can condensed vegetable soup
1 soup can water
1 (220-g) can baked beans in tomato sauce
Garnish
grated cheese

Empty the contents of the soup can into a saucepan and gradually stir in the water. Add the can of baked beans and heat, stirring gently, until almost boiling. Pour into hot soup bowls, sprinkle with cheese. Serve with crusty French bread and butter.
(Illustrated opposite)

IMPERIAL
1 (10½-oz) can condensed vegetable soup
1 soup can water
1 (7¾-oz) can baked beans in tomato sauce
Garnish
grated cheese

Bean chowder (see above)

MINUTE SAVERS

To make any cream or concentrated soup go further, add a chicken stock cube and a whole extra can of water.

When heating canned soups, bring only just up to the boil. Stir constantly too — over-boiling or scorching will spoil the flavour.

When using concentrated soups, empty the contents of the soup can into the saucepan first. Then with a wooden spoon slowly stir in the liquid and blend well before placing over the heat.

Whenever cream is added to a soup or sauce, re-check the seasoning because cream tends to mellow flavours. The reverse can be useful too, for the addition of cream will reduce the too strong taste of an over-seasoned recipe.

To make a very quick jellied consommé — make up a beef or chicken stock cube to 450 ml/¾ pint with a tablespoon aspic jelly crystals; add 1 tablespoon dry sherry and leave to cool. Stir with a fork when almost setting.

Melted aspic or consommé for glazing meat or poultry must be cold when used to get a good covering. A stir with a hot metal tablespoon will prevent it from actually setting up if it looks like doing so. Any left-over jelly should be allowed to set in a tin. Then chop it with a wet knife so

that the pieces remain separate and can be used as an attractive garnish.

To make hard butter soft for spreading quickly — beat in a little boiling water. Use 1 teaspoon for every 50 g/2 oz butter and blend thoroughly in a mixing basin.

To heat bread or rolls that are past the fresh stage for serving with snacks or salads, wrap in foil and place in a moderately hot oven (200°C, 400°F, Gas Mark 6); leave to heat through for 15-20 minutes. Keep wrapped in foil until ready to serve.

Check the seasoning of your dishes as you go along; it's better to alter the seasoning during cooking than to leave it until the dish is on the table.

Metal is a good conductor of heat and china or glass a poor one. Always place a metal baking tray under a pie or quiche in a china or ovenproof glass dish to help conduct the heat through to the pastry on the base.

Work tidily and you'll have less clearing up to do afterwards. Set a large paper carton or carrier bag beside where you are working and simply tip all peelings, cans and cartons into this. When you have finished cooking, clear away the box or bag.

DESSERTS

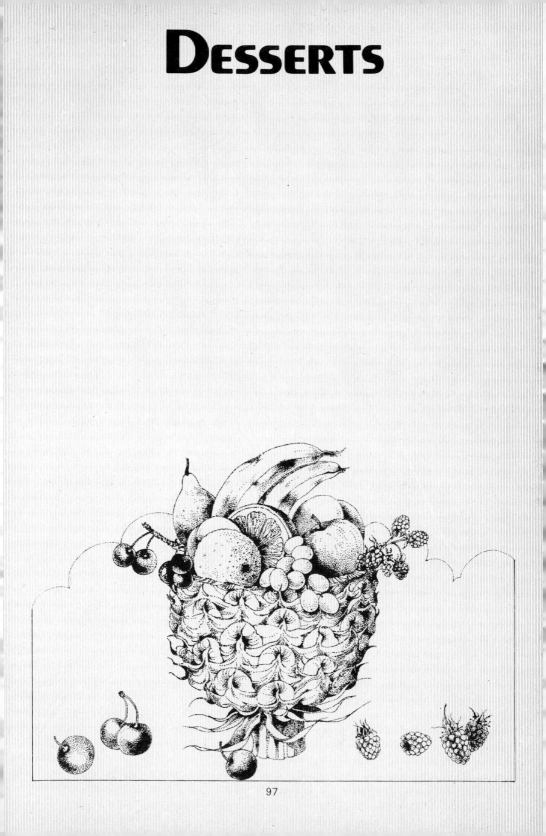

Deciding on a dessert is usually less difficult than choosing a main course. Ingredients are nearly always to hand in the store cupboard. Make sure you have cans of cream, evaporated milk, creamed rice and fruit and a good supply of glacé cherries, angelica and walnuts for pretty decorations.

Fresh fruit ideas

Some of the quickest and easiest desserts are made with fresh fruit; it's always a good idea to have plenty of apples, oranges and lemons in the house. Fresh fruit and cheese make an adequate dessert all the year round, but when citrus fruits are available in winter months it is nicer to turn them into something special.

Orange compote

Serves 6
Cooking time 6-7 minutes

METRIC	IMPERIAL
6 oranges	6 oranges
175 g castor sugar	6 oz castor sugar
150 ml water	$\frac{1}{4}$ pint water
juice of $\frac{1}{2}$ lemon	juice of $\frac{1}{2}$ lemon

Peel the oranges, keeping them whole and removing as much of the white pith as possible. Then using a sharp knife slice each orange across thinly. Arrange the slices in a serving dish and set aside to chill while preparing the syrup.

Measure the sugar and water into a saucepan. Stir over a low heat to dissolve the sugar. Bring to the boil and simmer for 1 minute. Draw off the heat and add the lemon juice. Allow to cool slightly. Pour the syrup over the oranges and leave until quite cold. Chill for several hours before serving.

Baked apples

Serves 4
Cooking time 45-50 minutes

METRIC	IMPERIAL
4 large, sharp-flavoured apples	4 large, sharp-flavoured apples
castor sugar (see method)	castor sugar (see method)
25 g butter	1 oz butter
3 tablespoons water	3 tablespoons water
150 ml single cream	$\frac{1}{4}$ pint single cream

Wash the apples and remove the cores keeping the apples whole. Using the tip of a sharp knife run the blade around the centre of the apple just to pierce the skin. Place the apples in a large roasting or baking tin. Fill the centre of each with sugar and top each apple with a flake of butter. Add the water to the tin and bake in a moderate oven (180°C, 350°F, Gas Mark 4), for 45-50 minutes.

When baked, the apples will puff up and become quite soft. Serve with the syrup from the tin and the single cream.

Orange fool

Serves 6

METRIC
3 medium oranges
1 lemon
75 g castor sugar
300 ml double cream
1 egg white

IMPERIAL
3 medium oranges
1 lemon
3 oz castor sugar
½ pint double cream
1 egg white

Finely grate the rind from the oranges and lemon into a small basin. Add the strained fruit juice and the sugar. Stir to dissolve the sugar in the fruit juices.

Pour the cream into a larger mixing basin and add the unbeaten egg white. Whisk the cream until thick and light, then using a metal spoon, fold in the orange and sugar liquid. At first the quantity of liquid may appear to be almost too much, but cut and fold through the cream, turning the basin to get a smooth, deliciously flavoured orange fool.

Pour into six individual glasses and chill for several hours when the mixture will take on a thick texture.

This is a good dessert for a dinner party as it can be made well in advance. Serve with sponge fingers.

Rum bananas

Serves 6
Cooking time about 5 minutes

METRIC
50 g butter
6 ripe bananas, peeled and cut in half lengthwise
50 g soft brown sugar
pinch of cinnamon
2-3 tablespoons rum

IMPERIAL
2 oz butter
6 ripe bananas, peeled and cut in half lengthwise
2 oz soft brown sugar
pinch of cinnamon
2-3 tablespoons rum

Melt the butter in a frying pan over a low heat. Add the bananas and sprinkle with the mixed sugar and cinnamon. Fry gently until the bananas are lightly browned, then turn. When the bananas are soft, add the rum, set alight and serve at once with the liquid from the pan spooned over.

Banana cream

Serves 4

METRIC
3 bananas
1 (142-ml) carton natural yogurt
50 g castor sugar
juice of ½ lemon
150 ml double cream
Decoration
few walnuts or grated chocolate

IMPERIAL
3 bananas
1 (5-fl oz) carton natural yogurt
2 oz castor sugar
juice of ½ lemon
¼ pint double cream
Decoration
few walnuts or grated chocolate

Mash the bananas in a small bowl, add the yogurt, sugar and lemon juice and mix together.

Whisk the cream until thick and fold into the mixture. Spoon into four individual serving glasses, top with finely chopped walnuts or grated chocolate and chill until ready to serve.

Apricot flummery

Serves 4
Cooking time 8-10 minutes

METRIC
1 (822-g) can apricot halves
about 2 tablespoons cornflour (see method)
juice of ½ lemon
Decoration
sliced almonds, toasted

IMPERIAL
1 (1 lb 13-oz) can apricot halves
about 2 tablespoons cornflour (see method)
juice of ½ lemon
Decoration
sliced almonds, toasted

Put apricots and juice through a sieve into a mixing bowl. Using a wooden spoon rub the fruit flesh through to get the maximum amount of purée. Discard any skin or hard flesh that will not pass through the sieve.

Measure the purée into a medium-sized saucepan and for each 300 ml/½ pint of mixture, measure 1 tablespoon cornflour into a small mixing bowl. Blend with cold water to a thin paste then stir into the apricot purée. Blending the cornflour in this way ensures that the mixture will not become lumpy when heated.

Transfer the mixture to a pan and gradually bring up to the boil, stirring constantly until thickened and clear. (All cornflour mixtures appear cloudy until the flour grains have cooked, then the mixture appears more clear and shiny. This should be apparent after simmering the mixture for about 1-2 minutes.)

Draw the pan off the heat and allow to cool, stirring occasionally to prevent a skin forming. Stir in the strained lemon juice and pour the mixture into four individual dessert dishes. Sprinkle the tops with toasted almonds and serve warm or chilled with cream or top of the milk.

Hot spiced peaches

Serves 6
Cooking time 15 minutes

METRIC
1 (825-g) can peach halves
50 g soft brown sugar
1 teaspoon cinnamon
300 ml single cream

IMPERIAL
1 (1 lb 13-oz) can peach halves
2 oz soft brown sugar
1 teaspoon cinnamon
½ pint single cream

Drain the peaches, reserving 150 ml/¼ pint of the juice. Arrange the peach halves, cut side up in a small baking or roasting tin. Pour the reserved juice into the base of the tin.

Combine together the brown sugar and cinnamon and sprinkle evenly over the peaches. Bake in a moderately hot oven (190°C, 375°F, Gas Mark 5) for 15 minutes. Serve at once with juices from the baking tin, and cream.

DESSERTS

PEACH MELBA

Serves 6
Cooking time 5-10 minutes

Turn the raspberries into a small mixing bowl, sprinkle over the sugar and set aside to thaw until the raspberries are soft and a juice forms. Spoon the raspberries into a small saucepan and blend the cornflour smoothly with the juice left in the bowl. Add to the raspberries in the saucepan, place over a low heat and bring to the boil, stirring continuously until thickened. Draw the pan off the heat and set aside, stirring occasionally, until cool.

Place a scoop of ice cream in six individual glasses and top with two peach halves, rounded side up, and pour over the raspberry sauce.

Serve with a pompadour wafer if liked.

METRIC
1 (227-g) packet frozen raspberries
25 g granulated sugar
2 teaspoons cornflour
1 (500-ml) block vanilla ice cream
1 (825-g) can peach halves, drained

IMPERIAL
1 (8-oz) packet frozen raspberries
1 oz granulated sugar
2 teaspoons cornflour
1 (17·6-fl oz) block vanilla ice cream
1 (1 lb 13-oz) can peach halves, drained

SAUTÉED BANANAS AND PINEAPPLE

Serves 4
Cooking time 5 minutes

Melt the butter in a medium-sized frying pan over a low heat. Peel the bananas, cut into 2·5-cm/1-inch chunks and add to the butter along with the pineapple chunks.

Sprinkle the mixed brown sugar and cinnamon over the top and place over a low heat – a high heat might caramelise the butter and sugar. Cook gently for about 5 minutes, turning the fruit occasionally with a wooden spoon, until thoroughly warmed through. Cooked banana turns brown and soft very quickly so serve immediately with a little of the sauce from the pan spooned over, and cream.

METRIC
50 g butter
3 medium-sized bananas
1 (432-g) can pineapple chunks, drained
50 g soft brown sugar
¼ teaspoon ground cinnamon
150 ml single cream

IMPERIAL
2 oz butter
3 medium-sized bananas
1 (15½-oz) can pineapple chunks, drained
2 oz soft brown sugar
¼ teaspoon ground cinnamon
¼ pint single cream

Hot pears with
ice cream

Serves 4
Cooking time 10 minutes

METRIC
50 g butter
50 g soft brown sugar
½ teaspoon ground cinnamon
¼ teaspoon ground nutmeg
¼ teaspoon ground ginger
1 (825-g) can pear halves
1 (500-ml) block vanilla ice cream

Measure the butter, sugar and spices into a frying pan; drain the pear halves and arrange over the top. Set aside until ready to serve. About 10 minutes before serving, place the pan over a moderate heat and simmer the pears gently for 5 minutes, then turn over and simmer for a further 5 minutes until heated through. Place a scoop of vanilla ice cream in four individual glasses and place two pear halves on top with a little of the hot sauce from the pan spooned over. Serve at once.

IMPERIAL
2 oz butter
2 oz soft brown sugar
½ teaspoon ground cinnamon
¼ teaspoon ground nutmeg
¼ teaspoon ground ginger
1 (1 lb 13-oz) can pear halves
1 (17·6-fl oz) block vanilla ice cream

Gingered pears

Serves 4
Cooking time 5-10 minutes

METRIC
50 g crystallised ginger
150 ml water
75 g castor sugar
juice of ½ lemon
1 (825-g) can pear halves
Decoration
chopped angelica and halved glacé cherries

Rinse the sugar coating off the ginger under warm water and then chop the ginger finely. Measure the water, sugar and lemon juice into a medium-sized saucepan and stir over a low heat to dissolve the sugar.

When making syrup for fruit all the sugar crystals must first be dissolved before boiling the mixture, otherwise the sugar grains will crystallise around the edge of the saucepan and make the finished texture of the syrup grainy. Add the chopped ginger to the syrup and bring up to the boil. Reduce the heat and simmer gently for 5-10 minutes to make a syrupy sauce.

Meanwhile drain the pears from the can, reserving the juice. Place the pears in a glass serving dish. Draw the boiling syrup off the heat and add the pear juice. Allow to cool, then pour over the pears. Sprinkle with the angelica and cherries and chill very thoroughly before serving.

IMPERIAL
2 oz crystallised ginger
¼ pint water
3 oz castor sugar
juice of ½ lemon
1 (1 lb 13-oz) can pear halves
Decoration
chopped angelica and halved glacé cherries

Sweets – light and airy

Quick mousses, jellies and ice cream desserts can be prepared ahead and left to chill. Use packet jellies as a base for some recipes. For others with gelatine, avoid using too many basins by soaking and dissolving the gelatine powder in a fairly large saucepan, then stirring or folding in the other ingredients. Use instant whip for quick trifles or vary them by folding in fruit purée to make fruit fools, or whipped cream, chocolate or nuts to make easy desserts.

Orange and banana jelly

Serves 4-6

METRIC
orange squash (see method)
water (see method)
15 g powdered gelatine
2 bananas

IMPERIAL
orange squash (see method)
water (see method)
½ oz powdered gelatine
2 bananas

Dilute the orange squash with water to taste, making up 600 ml/1 pint of liquid. Measure the powdered gelatine into a saucepan, add 150 ml/¼ pint of the liquid and allow to soak for 5 minutes. Place the saucepan over a very low heat and stir to dissolve the gelatine. Draw the pan off the heat and add the remaining liquid. Pour the jelly into a serving dish and chill until almost set.

Quickly slice the bananas and stir into the jelly, then leave until firmly set.

Banana mousse

Serves 4-6

METRIC
300 ml water
1 packet greengage or lime jelly
3 large bananas
juice of ½ lemon
300 ml double cream
Decoration
toasted almonds or grated chocolate

IMPERIAL
½ pint water
1 packet greengage or lime jelly
3 large bananas
juice of ½ lemon
½ pint double cream
Decoration
toasted almonds or grated chocolate

Measure 150 ml/¼ pint of the water into a saucepan, bring up to the boil and then draw off the heat. Add the jelly in pieces and stir until dissolved – the heat of the pan is sufficient to do this. When the jelly is dissolved, stir in the remaining cold water and set aside until cooled and beginning to thicken.

Meanwhile peel and mash the bananas with the lemon juice. Whisk the cream until thick and then fold into the almost-set jelly along with the mashed banana. Pour into a serving dish and leave until set. Sprinkle with almonds or chocolate and serve.

Quick
chocolate mousse

Serves 4

METRIC
100 g plain chocolate
15 g butter
4 eggs, separated

Break the chocolate into a mixing bowl and set over a pan of hot water. Stir until melted and smooth, then add the butter and egg yolks. Stir until blended then remove the bowl from heat. Stiffly whisk the egg whites and fold them carefully into the chocolate mixture. Spoon into four individual serving glasses and chill until set firm — this takes 1-2 hours.

IMPERIAL
4 oz plain chocolate
$\frac{1}{2}$ oz butter
4 eggs, separated

Swiss cream

Serves 6

- METRIC
1 packet greengage jelly
300 ml water
1 banana, sliced
few pieces of angelica
1 jam-filled Swiss roll
1 small can evaporated milk
1 tablespoon lemon juice

Dissolve the jelly in hot water to make 300 ml/$\frac{1}{2}$ pint, then allow to cool until just warm. Pour enough into a 15-cm/6-inch deep cake tin to cover the base and leave to set.

Arrange the banana slices and the pieces of angelica over the set jelly in a decorative pattern. Spoon over a little more jelly and leave to set. Slice the Swiss roll into eight and dip each slice cut side down, into the remaining jelly. Place the slices, jelly-coated sides outside, around the edge of the tin. Press well against the sides of the tin and leave to set.

Beat the evaporated milk and lemon juice together until thick. Gradually beat in the remainder of the jelly which should be almost set by now.

Pour this mixture into the centre of the prepared tin and leave in a cool place until set quite firm. Unmould carefully on to a plate and serve with cream.

IMPERIAL
1 packet greengage jelly
$\frac{1}{2}$ pint water
1 banana, sliced
few pieces of angelica
1 jam-filled Swiss roll
1 small can evaporated milk
1 tablespoon lemon juice

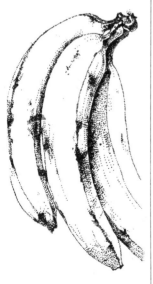

LEMON CRUMB FREEZE

Serves 8

METRIC
50 g cornflakes, crushed
50 g castor sugar
50 g butter or margarine, melted
2 eggs, separated
1 small can condensed milk
150 ml double cream
finely grated rind and juice of 2 lemons
25 g castor sugar

Measure the crumbs into a medium-sized bowl and add the sugar; using a fork, stir in the melted fat until all the crumbs are coated. Reserving 2 tablespoons of the crumb mixture for the top, pat the remainder out firmly on the base of an ice cube tray (use a large ice tray, if possible) previously lined with a strip of waxed paper. Set aside to chill while preparing the filling.

Combine together the egg yolks, condensed milk and cream. Add the lemon rind and strained juice and stir until thickened.

Beat the egg whites until foamy and whisk in the sugar. Fold gently into the lemon mixture and pour over the base of crumbs in the ice cube tray. Sprinkle the reserved crumble over the lemon mixture and freeze for 2-3 hours until firm. To serve, loosen the sides, lift out the dessert and cut in slices.

IMPERIAL
2 oz cornflakes, crushed
2 oz castor sugar
2 oz butter or margarine melted
2 eggs, separated
1 small can condensed milk
¼ pint double cream
finely grated rind and juice of 2 lemons
1 oz castor sugar

GINGER CREAM ROLL

Serves 6

METRIC
1 (200-g) packet ginger snaps
300 ml double cream
1 teaspoon vanilla essence
Decoration
chopped candied ginger

Unwrap the ginger snaps and set aside any broken ones. Whip the cream and vanilla essence until thick and using half the cream spread on the ginger snaps and pile on top of each other. Lay the roll on its side in a serving dish, spoon the remaining cream over and with the tip of a knife spread evenly to cover.

Set aside to chill in a refrigerator for at least 3-4 hours to allow the biscuits to soften before serving. Sprinkle with candied ginger and serve sliced diagonally.

IMPERIAL
1 (7·05-oz) packet ginger snaps
½ pint double cream
1 teaspoon vanilla essence
Decoration
chopped candied ginger

Easy lemon soufflé

Serves 4-6

METRIC		IMPERIAL
water (see method)		water (see method)
1 packet lemon jelly		1 packet lemon jelly
finely grated rind and juice of 1 lemon		finely grated rind and juice of 1 lemon
1 large can evaporated milk		1 large can evaporated milk
150 ml double cream		$\frac{1}{4}$ pint double cream
Decoration		*Decoration*
chopped walnuts		chopped walnuts

Measure 150 ml/$\frac{1}{4}$ pint cold water into a saucepan and bring up to the boil. Draw the pan off the heat and add the jelly in pieces. Stir until dissolved — it is not necessary to replace the pan over the heat. Make the dissolved jelly up to 300 ml/$\frac{1}{2}$ pint with cold water, using about 3 tablespoons extra water. Add the lemon rind and set aside until cooled and almost beginning to set.

Whisk the evaporated milk — use it from a chilled can if possible — and strained lemon juice together until thick and light. Then gradually whisk in the jelly. Continue to beat until the mixture begins to thicken, then quickly fold in the cream and pour the mixture into a serving dish. Sprinkle with chopped walnuts and leave aside until set.

Quick ideas

Peach crumb whip Cut any left-over cake, icing as well, into cubes. Add cubed canned peaches, coarsely chopped nuts and fold into lightly whipped cream. Chill before serving.

Orange-baked peaches Combine equal amounts of orange juice and peach syrup with a little grated orange rind, brown sugar, whole cloves and butter. Pour over canned peach halves in shallow baking pan. Bake in a moderate oven (180°C, 350°F, Gas Mark 4) for 15 minutes. Serve warm with cream.

Rice and raspberries Empty the contents of a large can of creamed rice into a basin and fold in 150 ml/$\frac{1}{4}$ pint whipped double cream and a packet of thawed frozen raspberries. Sweeten if necessary.

Fruit and shortbread fingers To any drained canned fruit syrup, add a little sherry or brandy. Pour over the fruit and serve fruit topped with whipped cream. Hand round shortbread fingers separately.

Fruit fool Stir 4-5 tablespoons condensed milk into 300 ml/$\frac{1}{2}$ pint unsweetened fruit purée (blackcurrant is particularly delicious). Serve in individual glass dishes and hand round sponge fingers.

Peach mallow Fill canned peach halves with chopped canned pineapple. Top with snipped marshmallows and put under a hot grill until the marshmallows turn golden brown. Serve hot.

Butterscotch crunch Prepare instant butterscotch pudding according to instructions on the packet. When it is beginning to set, fold in 150 ml/$\frac{1}{4}$ pint whipped double cream. Spoon into serving glasses and top with crushed peanut brittle.

Easy trifle Line a dish with broken sponge fingers and spinkle with chopped glacé cherries. Pour in prepared instant pudding. When it is set, decorate the top with whipped double cream and walnuts.

Old-fashioned chocolate pudding Prepare instant chocolate dessert according to the instructions on the packet. Pour into individual serving dishes and top with brown sugar and finely chopped walnuts. Serve with single cream.

Fruit cream Pour a prepared instant whip over either cut-up orange sections or canned pineapple chunks and sliced banana. Chill before serving.

Grape cocktail Halve and de-seed 225 g/8 oz green grapes. Divide equally between four serving glasses and sprinkle with sweet sherry. Top with a spoonful of soured cream and a sprinkling of brown sugar.

DESSERTS

Rice sundae Drain the contents of a can of fruit cocktail and spoon alternate layers of fruit and canned creamed rice into individual serving glasses. Top with whipped double cream and chopped nuts — for extra flavour add 1 tablespoon brandy to the cream before whipping.

Quick coffee rice Dissolve $\frac{1}{2}$ teaspoon instant coffee powder in a little hot water and stir in the contents of a 454-g/1-lb can of creamed rice. Spoon into four individual serving dishes and top with whipped double cream and chopped walnuts.

Iced white peaches Empty the contents of a 425-g/15-oz can of white peaches into a serving dish; chill until ready to serve.

Banana tango Slice banana and cover with canned orange juice.

Pears in port Drain canned pear halves. Pour over sufficient port to cover and chill until ready to serve.

Caramelised pears Sprinkle drained canned pear halves with lemon juice, then with melted butter and a little brown sugar and ground nutmeg or cinnamon. Grill for about 8 minutes, or until golden. Serve topped with soft vanilla ice cream.

Pineapple sauté Sauté canned pineapple slices or peach halves in butter until golden. Serve topped with ice cream, then with some of the fruit syrup and if liked a touch of sherry.

Jelly jumble Prepare a fruit jelly and when firm run a fork through it. Pile on canned pineapple or fruit cocktail.

Snow-capped plums Top canned purple plums with a generous spoonful of soured cream and a little grated nutmeg.

Plum medley Combine a can each of purple plums and greengage plums; add a little lemon juice and a pinch of ground mace.

Frosty peaches Top frozen or canned peach slices with the following ice cream sauce. Stir 600 ml/1 pint vanilla ice cream until soft, but not runny. Add a few drops of almond essence.

Hot peaches Heat canned peaches or fruit cocktail, including the juice, with a little lemon peel. Serve as it is, or on top of vanilla ice cream.

Continental platter Serve fresh oranges and cheese as a dessert.

Frosted strawberries Top thawed frozen sliced strawberries with soured cream, then a sprinkling of brown sugar.

MINUTE SAVERS

Beaten egg whites break down if left to stand — so only whip them just before adding to the recipe.

Eggs separate more easily when taken straight from the refrigerator, but whites beat up to a better volume when at room temperature.

Beat equal quantities of double and single cream together to make a light consistency that is best for piping. Double cream whipped on its own tends to over-thicken owing to the pressure used to force it through a piping bag and can separate.

Rinse a saucepan with cold water before heating milk or making custards. This makes cleaning easier.

Always fold a cuff back on the large cotton or nylon piping bags before spooning in mashed potato, meringue mixture or cream for piping. This automatically prevents over-filling. Fold the cuff back up and twist it closed for piping. No filling will leak out at the top this way.

Add any flavouring or sugar to double cream before whisking up, not afterwards. This reduces the risk of over-beating.

To make a plain jelly set quickly, dissolve the jelly in half quantity of boiling water. Make up with ice cubes and by the time the cubes have melted the jelly will be almost setting.

Only the outer rind or zest of citrus fruits contains the essential flavouring oils. Rubbing lump sugar over the surface is one method of absorbing the true flavour for dessert recipes but a fine grater will do the job as well so long as the bitter white pith underneath is not included.

Before squeezing a lemon, roll it between the hands to warm a little. You'll find the juice will flow more easily.

Immerse a moulded gelatine dessert up to the rim in water no hotter than the hand can bear comfortably – otherwise the outside of the mould melts giving a blurred appearance. Count up to ten then lift out and shake the mould in the hand to allow the air to get down the sides before turning out onto a plate. Try wetting the serving plate with a little cold water. Then if the dessert unmoulds a little off centre, you can coax it into position without spoiling its shape

Ingredients will combine perfectly if they are of a similar consistency. So all gelatine mixtures should be allowed to cool until beginning to thicken before any beaten egg whites or whipped cream are folded in. Then you get a better volume.

Stand a dessert mould in a baking or roasting tin and surround with ice cubes when fixing a jelly layer on the base. This way it sets up very quickly. Don't forget to set any fruit decoration with a little extra jelly or it will move when you pour in the filling.

A smart cook stores one or two vanilla pods in a jar of castor sugar and the flavour will permeate through the grains to make vanilla sugar. Use this to flavour cakes and sweeten puddings in place of vanilla essence and you will find recipes have a subtle, more pleasant flavour. The same pods can be infused in milk to flavour custards, then dried and replaced in the jar. Top up the jar with extra sugar as it is used.

Quick breads, cakes and pastry

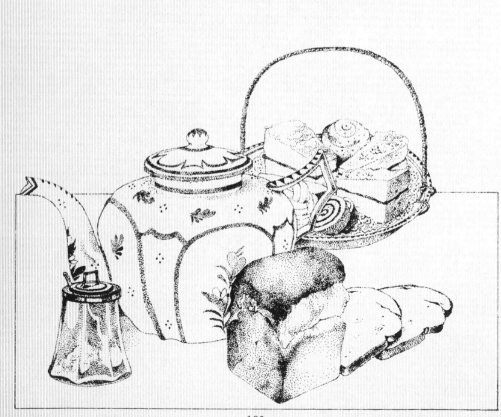

Quick breads, raised with baking powder, a modern easy-mix method for mixing cakes and home-made pastry mixes to store in the refrigerator make it possible for even the busiest of cooks to bake at week-ends.

The term quick bread nearly always applies to fruit breads or easy plain loaves risen with baking powder or a mixture of cream of tartar and bicarbonate of soda. Rich fruity breads keep well but plainer breads should be eaten fresh.

For simple yeast breads any cook can keep a tin of dried yeast in the store cupboard. Dried yeast is very easy to use and can replace the fresh yeast in any recipe. If using dried yeast in a recipe that lists fresh yeast, always use half the quantity of dried yeast and remember that 1 tablespoon dried yeast equals 15 g/$\frac{1}{2}$ oz or is the equivalent to 30 g/1 oz fresh yeast.

Simple yeast breads and rolls can be made more quickly by proving only once after the dough has been shaped. Although generally accepted that this method does not give as good a texture as the traditional method of proving or rising twice, it's very satisfactory for simple little recipes. When the dough is proved only once, to get a good rise when baking the dough must be very thoroughly kneaded to develop the gluten in the flour.

The best kind of tins for baking fruit breads are plain loaf tins in preference to bread tins; they are not so deep and make fruit breads a more attractive shape. When preparing for use grease well then line with a strip of grease proof paper cut to the width of the pan and long enough to cover the base and two opposite ends of the tin — it's not necessary to line the sides.

New soft margarines, which spread straight from the refrigerator enable you to make a variety of quick, all-in-one cakes and biscuits which save time in both mixing and washing up.

Quick plain loaf

Cooking time 30-35 minutes

METRIC		IMPERIAL
400 g self-raising flour		1 lb self-raising flour
1 teaspoon salt		1 teaspoon salt
200 ml milk		$\frac{1}{2}$ pint milk

Sift the flour and salt into a mixing bowl. Using a fork stir in the milk and mix to a rough dough. Turn out on to a lightly floured working surface and knead to a round about 2·5 cm/1 inch thick.

Place on a baking tray, dredged with flour, and bake in the centre of a moderately hot oven (190°C, 375°F, Gas Mark 5) for 30-35 minutes.

This bread is best eaten within a day.

Fruit tea bread

Cooking time 1$\frac{1}{2}$ hours

METRIC		IMPERIAL
275 g mixed sultanas and seedless raisins		10 oz mixed sultanas and seedless raisins
200 g soft brown sugar		7 oz soft brown sugar
300 ml cold tea without milk		$\frac{1}{2}$ pint cold tea without milk
1 large egg		1 large egg
275 g self-raising flour (or use self-raising wholemeal flour, usually to be found at health food stores)		10 oz self-raising flour (or use self-raising wholemeal flour, usually to be found at health food stores)

Measure the sultanas, raisins and brown sugar into a bowl. Pour over the cold tea and leave overnight. The dried fruit will soak up the tea to become plump and juicy, making a deliciously moist loaf.

Next day stir the ingredients once or twice, then lightly mix the egg and add with the flour. Using a wooden spoon mix well until smooth. Pour into a well-greased 1-kg/2-lb loaf tin which has been lined with a strip of greaseproof paper cut to cover the base and overlap the two ends. Spread the mixture level. Bake in the centre of a moderate oven (180°C, 350°F, Gas Mark 4) for 1$\frac{1}{2}$ hours.

(Illustrated opposite)

Fruit tea bread (see above)

Hot seed rolls

Makes 18
Cooking time 15 minutes

METRIC
450 g self-raising flour
2 teasoons baking powder
1 teaspoon salt
100 g butter or margarine
200 ml milk
milk for brushing
caraway or sesame seeds

IMPERIAL
1 lb self-raising flour
2 teaspoons baking powder
1 teaspoon salt
4 oz butter or margarine
$\frac{1}{3}$ pint milk
milk for brushing
caraway or sesame seeds

Sift the flour, baking powder and salt into a large mixing bowl. Add the fat in pieces and rub into the mixture thoroughly to distribute the fat evenly. Hollow out a well in the dry ingredients and pour all the milk into the centre. Using a fork for easiest handling, blend quickly to a rough dough. Turn on to a lightly floured working surface and knead to a smooth dough — add only enough flour to prevent dough sticking to the table.

Divide the dough into three portions and then divide each portion into six smaller pieces. With floured hands — this way the dough will not stick to your fingers — roll each piece out to a rope about 15-18 cm/6-7 inches long. Tie each of the first six pieces of dough into a simple knot. Place on a greased baking tray, brush with milk and sprinkle with seeds.

Roll the next six into whorls — starting at one end, simply roll the rope of dough back along itself. Place flat on a greased baking tray, brush with milk and sprinkle with cosame seeds

Shape the last six pieces of dough into loops. Turn each end into the centre and then draw ends up together. Place flat on a greased baking tray, brush with milk and sprinkle with caraway seeds.

Bake above the centre of a hot oven (220°C, 425°F, Gas Mark 7) for 15 minutes, until browned. If rolls are on two trays, place one on a lower shelf, moving up to the top when first tray is baked, for further 5 minutes browning.

These rolls are nicest served warm.

Victoria sandwich (see page 114)

All-in-one cakes

Using a quick all-in-one method, the ingredients for the cake are blended thoroughly for one minute only and the mixture is ready for baking. It's a new idea and has proved a very successful one. This method cannot be used for any cake recipe since the proportions have to be carefully worked out. For instance, most all-in-one recipes use self-raising flour with added baking powder — this gives the extra rise, since, without the long creaming process normally used, less air is incorporated.

All ingredients must be at room temperature; this applies particularly to the margarine, eggs and milk — and it's important that none of these are used straight from the refrigerator. Quick creaming margarines are most satisfactory, as the fat blends in evenly with the other ingredients. Never use butter which, although ideal in normal cake recipes, is too hard a fat for all-in-one cakes.

Cream-filled sandwich cake

Cooking time 25-30 minutes

METRIC		IMPERIAL
125 g self-raising flour		4 oz self-raising flour
1 teaspoon baking powder		1 teaspoon baking powder
125 g castor sugar		4 oz castor sugar
125 g soft margarine		4 oz soft margarine
2 large eggs		2 large eggs
vanilla essence		vanilla essence
2 tablespoons raspberry jam		2 tablespoons raspberry jam
Filling		*Filling*
50 g soft margarine		2 oz soft margarine
50 g castor sugar		2 oz castor sugar
6 teaspoons hot water		6 teaspoons hot water
4 teaspoons cold milk		4 teaspoons cold milk
Topping		*Topping*
icing sugar		icing sugar

Sift the flour and baking powder into a large mixing bowl. Add the sugar, margarine, cut in slices, eggs and a few drops of vanilla essence. Mix the ingredients thoroughly and beat with a wooden spoon for 1 minute.

Dividing the mixture evenly, spoon into two greased and lined 18-cm/7-inch sponge cake tins. Bake in the centre of a moderate oven (180°C, 350°F, Gas Mark 4) for 25-30 minutes, or until risen and firm to the touch. Remove from the tins and allow to cool on a wire tray.

For the filling — cream together the sugar and margarine until light. Beat in the hot water 1 teaspoon at a time. At this stage the mixture will be very soft. Gradually add the milk, beating very thoroughly between each addition.

To finish the cake — when cool, spread the base of one layer with raspberry jam. Spoon on the cream filling to cover the jam. Top with the remaining cake layer and dust with sifted icing sugar.

Variation

Victoria sandwich Omit the cream in the filling, and use raspberry jam. Dust with sifted icing sugar. *(Illustrated on page 112)*

Swiss roll

Cooking time 15-20 minutes

METRIC
125 g self-raising flour
1 teaspoon baking powder
125 g castor sugar
125 g soft margarine
2 large eggs
little castor sugar
300 ml double cream
Topping
little icing sugar

Sift the flour and baking powder into a large mixing bowl. Add the sugar, margarine, cut in slices, and eggs. Mix thoroughly and then beat with a wooden spoon for 1 minute.

Spoon the mixture into a greased and lined Swiss roll tin. Spread the mixture evenly — particularly in the corners of the tin. Bake in the centre of a moderately hot oven (190°C, 375°F, Gas Mark 5) for 15-20 minutes, or until evenly risen and brown. Immediately the Swiss roll is baked turn it out on to a sheet of greaseproof paper, previously sprinkled with castor sugar. Using a knife trim away the edges and roll up, leaving the paper inside. Leave to cool.

Whip the cream until thick, then finish the Swiss roll; very gently unroll, only enough to remove the greaseproof paper. Using a knife, spread the cream over the inside of the sponge and quickly re-roll again. Sprinkle with icing sugar and cut in slices.

IMPERIAL
4 oz self-raising flour
1 teaspoon baking powder
4 oz castor sugar
4 oz soft margarine
2 large eggs
little castor sugar
½ pint double cream
Topping
little icing sugar

CinnAmon spice cAke

Cooking time 25-30 minutes

METRIC
125 g self-raising flour
1½ teaspoons cinnamon
1 teaspoon baking powder
125 g castor sugar
125 g soft margarine
2 eggs
little icing sugar
Filling
100 g icing sugar
1½ teaspoons cinnamon
50 g soft margarine
2 teaspoons milk
Topping
icing sugar

Sift the flour, cinnamon and baking powder into a large mixing bowl. Add the sugar, margarine, cut in slices, and eggs. Mix thoroughly and then beat with a wooden spoon for 1 minute.

Dividing the mixture evenly, spoon into two greased and lined 18-cm/7-inch sandwich cake tins. Smooth the tops and bake in the centre of a moderate oven (180°C, 350°F, Gas Mark 4) for 20-25 minutes. Allow to cool before filling.

Sift the icing sugar and cinnamon into a small mixing bowl. Add the margarine and milk and then beat together until thoroughly mixed. Sandwich the two layer cakes with the filling and dust the top with a little sifted icing sugar.

IMPERIAL
4 oz self-raising flour
1½ teaspoons cinnamon
1 teaspoon baking powder
4 oz castor sugar
4 oz soft margarine
2 eggs
little icing sugar
Filling
4 oz icing sugar
1½ teaspoons cinnamon
2 oz soft margarine
2 teaspoons milk
Topping
icing sugar

Mocha gâteau

Cooking time 20-25 minutes

METRIC	IMPERIAL
150 g self-raising flour	5 oz self-raising flour
pinch of salt	pinch of salt
pinch of bicarbonate of soda	pinch of bicarbonate of soda
1 teaspoon baking powder	1 teaspoon baking powder
25 g cocoa powder	1 oz cocoa powder
100 g castor sugar	4 oz castor sugar
100 g soft margarine	4 oz soft margarine
1 tablespoon golden syrup	1 tablespoon golden syrup
2 eggs	2 eggs
3 tablespoons milk	3 tablespoons milk
1 teaspoon coffee essence	1 teaspoon coffee essence
coffee butter cream (see page 117)	coffee butter cream (see page 117)
Topping	*Topping*
icing sugar	icing sugar

Sift the flour, salt, bicarbonate of soda, baking powder and cocoa powder together into a large mixing bowl. Add all remaining ingredients, slicing the margarine. Mix together thoroughly and then using a wooden spoon beat well for 1 minute. Divide the mixture equally between two greased and lined 18-cm/7-inch sandwich tins. Spread the mixture level and bake in the centre of a moderate oven (180°C, 350°F, Gas Mark 4) for 20-25 minutes.

Cool and then sandwich together with coffee butter cream. Dust with sifted icing sugar.

Frosted coconut cake

Cooking time 20-25 minutes

METRIC	IMPERIAL
150 g self-raising flour	5 oz self-raising flour
1½ teaspoons baking powder	1½ teaspoons baking powder
40 g desiccated coconut	1½ oz desiccated coconut
100 g castor sugar	4 oz castor sugar
100 g soft margarine	4 oz soft margarine
2 large eggs	2 large eggs
2 tablespoons milk	2 tablespoons milk
¼ teaspoon vanilla essence	¼ teaspoon vanilla essence
quick vanilla butter cream (see page 117)	quick vanilla butter cream (see page 117)
vanilla glacé icing (see page 117)	vanilla glacé icing (see page 117)
Decoration	*Decoration*
desiccated coconut	desiccated coconut

Sift the flour and baking powder into a large mixing bowl. Add all the remaining ingredients, slicing the margarine. Mix thoroughly then beat with a wooden spoon for 1 minute. Dividing the mixture equally, spoon into two greased and lined 18-cm/7-inch sandwich cake tins. Bake in the centre of a moderately hot oven (190°C, 375°F, Gas Mark 5) for 20-25 minutes, or until risen and firm to the touch.

To finish the cake, sandwich with vanilla-flavoured butter cream, coloured a delicate pink. Coat the top with the palest pink vanilla glacé icing and sprinkle with desiccated coconut, whilst the icing is still wet.

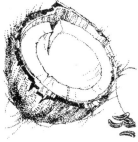

Quick vanilla butter cream

To fill and top one 18-cm/7-inch or
20-cm/8-inch sandwich cake

METRIC		IMPERIAL
75 g soft margarine		3 oz soft margarine
225 g icing sugar		8 oz icing sugar
4 teaspoons milk		4 teaspoons milk
½ teaspoon vanilla essence		½ teaspoon vanilla essence
food colouring (optional)		food colouring (optional)

Place all the ingredients in a mixing bowl and beat together with a wooden spoon until well mixed — this takes 2-3 minutes. Add food colouring if required.

Variations

Chocolate butter cream Omit the vanilla essence; blend 1½ tablespoons cocoa powder with 2 tablespoons hot water and cool. Omit the milk in the recipe and use this chocolate liquid.

Coffee butter cream Omit the vanilla essence; replace 2 teaspoons milk with 2 teaspoons coffee essence.

Orange butter cream Omit the vanilla essence; replace 4 teaspoons milk with 4 teaspoons orange juice plus a little food colouring.

Lemon butter cream Omit the vanilla essence; replace 4 teaspoons milk with 4 teaspoons lemon juice plus a little food colouring.

Vanilla glacé icing

To cover top and sides of two
18-cm/7-inch or 20-cm/8-inch cakes

METRIC		IMPERIAL
225 g icing sugar		8 oz icing sugar
2-3 tablespoons hot water		2-3 tablespoons hot water
few drops of vanilla essence		few drops of vanilla essence
food colouring (optional)		food colouring (optional)

Sift the icing sugar into a mixing bowl. Stir in the hot water — this makes the icing set more quickly — and the vanilla essence. Add a few drops of food colouring if required for a particular recipe. Pour immediately over the top of the cake and using a knife spread evenly over the top and sides.

Make your own ready-mix for pastry, scones and cakes

Cut out the long job of rubbing fat into flour every time pastry, scones or plain cakes are baked by preparing some of your own ready-mixes. They are very convenient to use as you just weigh out a quantity and add liquid. Store the dry rubbed-in mixture in closed polythene bags, plastic containers with airtight lids or screw-topped jars, each clearly labelled and dated. They will keep for up to 3 months in a refrigerator.

Just remember that pastry and cake mixes have half as much fat as flour. In a recipe calling for 225 g/8 oz flour and 125 g/4 oz fat, use 350 g/12 oz mix.

For pastry, allow about 1 teaspoon of water for every 35 g/1¼ oz dry mix. Use 175 g/6 oz pastry mix to cover a 1-litre/1½-pint pie dish or line an 18-cm/7-inch flan ring. Use 250 g/9 oz pastry mix to cover a 1·5-litre/2½-pint pie dish, to line a 20-cm/8-inch flan ring, or to make 8-12 tarts, cut with a 6-cm/2½-inch cutter. Use 350 g/12 oz pastry mix for a pie with pastry top and bottom. The mixes can be used straight from the refrigerator.

Pastry mix

Makes about 2 kg/4½ lb mix

METRIC		IMPERIAL
1·4 kg plain flour	Sift the flour and salt into a mixing bowl. Rub in the fats with the fingertips until the mixture resembles fine breadcrumbs. Store in a closed polythene bag, plastic container with an airtight lid or a screw-topped jar, in a refrigerator or cool dark place.	3 lb plain flour
3 teaspoons salt		3 teaspoons salt
350 g vegetable fat or lard		12 oz vegetable fat or lard
350 g margarine		12 oz margarine

Variations

Shortcrust pastry To 350 g/12 oz mix, add about 2-3 tablespoons cold water.

Sweet shortcrust To 350 g/12 oz mix, add 1 tablespoon castor sugar, 1 beaten egg and about 1 tablespoon cold water.

Savoury crumble topping To 175 g/6 oz mix, add ¼ teaspoon dried mixed herbs and 2-3 tablespoons cold water. Use to cover meat or fish mixtures. This makes enough for a 1-litre/1½-2-pint dish.

Cheese pastry To 350 g/12 oz mix, add ½ teaspoon dry mustard, pinch of cayenne pepper, 50 g/2 oz finely grated cheese and 2-3 tablespoons cold water.

Cake mix

Makes about 2 kg/4½ lb mix

METRIC
1·4 kg self-raising flour
3 teaspoons salt
675 g margarine

Sift the flour and salt into a mixing bowl. Rub in the margarine with fingertips until the mixture resembles fine breadcrumbs. Store in a closed polythene bag, plastic container with an airtight lid or a screw-topped jar, in a refrigerator or cool dark place.

IMPERIAL
3 lb self-raising flour
3 teaspoons salt
1½ lb margarine

Variations

Apricot buns To 275 g/10 oz mix, add 50 g/2 oz castor sugar, 1 beaten egg, 2 teaspoons milk, and mix to a stiff dough. Put 2 teaspoons of the mixture into each bun tin, make a hole in the centre with a spoon handle and drop in a little apricot jam. Bake in a moderately hot oven (200°C, 400°F, Gas Mark 6) for 15-20 minutes. *Makes 12.*

Fruit cake To 350 g/12 oz mix, add 100 g/4 oz castor sugar, 100 g/4 oz mixed fruit, 2 beaten eggs and 2-3 tablespoons milk. Mix to a stiff dropping consistency. Place in a lined and greased 15-cm/6-inch cake tin and bake in a moderate oven (160°C, 325°F, Gas Mark 3) for 1½ hours.

Spiced currant biscuits To 175 g/6 oz mix, add 25 g/1 oz castor sugar, 1 teaspoon cinnamon, 50 g/2 oz currants. 1 egg yolk and 2 teaspoons milk. Work together, then knead until smooth. Roll out to a 20-cm/8-inch circle, 5 mm/¼ inch thick. Cut into 12 triangles. Bake in a moderate oven (180°C, 350°F, Gas Mark 4) for 30 minutes.

Currant cakes To 350 g/12 oz of the mix add 75 g/3 oz castor sugar, 75 g/3 oz currants and mix to a soft dropping consistency with 1 egg lightly mixed with 5-6 tablespoons milk. Spoon into 24 paper cases placed in bun tins and bake above the centre in a moderately hot oven (190°C, 375°F, Gas Mark 5) for 25-30 minutes, until golden brown and springy to the touch.

Orange cakes Omit the fruit from the recipe above; add ½ teaspoon vanilla essence, grated rind of 1 orange and ¼ teaspoon orange essence; ice when cooled with glacé icing made with the orange juice.

SCONE MIX

Makes about 1·75 kg/4 lb mix

METRIC
1·4 kg self-raising flour
3 teaspoons salt
450g margarine

Sift the flour and salt into a mixing bowl. Rub in the margarine until the mixture resembles fine breadcrumbs. Store in a closed polythene bag, plastic container with an airtight lid or screw-topped jar, in a refrigerator or cool dark place.

IMPERIAL
3 lb self-raising flour
3 teaspoons salt
1 lb margarine

Variations

Sweet scones To 350 g/12 oz mix, add 25 g/1 oz castor sugar and about 150 ml/$\frac{1}{4}$ pint milk. Bake in a hot oven (220°C, 425°F, Gas Mark 7) for about 10 minutes.

Cheese scones To 350 g/12 oz mix, add 75 g/3 oz grated cheese and about 150 ml/$\frac{1}{4}$ pint milk. Bake in a hot oven (220°C, 425°F, Gas Mark 7) for about 10 minutes.

MINUTE SAVERS

Arrowroot cooks to a clear glaze so use it instead of cornflour to thicken juices for open fruit flans or tartlets. 1 teaspoon blended in a little cold water is the right amount for 150 ml/$\frac{1}{4}$ pint fruit juice. Stir over the heat until boiling and then use immediately.

Always wash floury pastry boards and rolling pins in cold water first – hot water makes the flour stick.

To encourage a bread dough to rise more quickly, place the tin or bowl of dough inside a large polythene bag and close the neck. Then set in a warm place – the dampness and warmth kept inside speeds up the rising.

Use lightly floured hands to shape scone or bread doughs, this helps prevent the mixture sticking to your fingers.

Measure out ingredients and preheat the oven before starting on all-in-one cake or bread recipes – those with raising agent added should be mixed quickly and put in the oven immediately for the best results.

Keep lots of ready-cut paper liners for tins in a kitchen drawer; it's easy to cut out several at one time and less wasteful too.

The professional touch

A clever cook always presents her food looking attractive and appetising. However simple the recipe may be, the use of herbs and seasonings or a garnish all help to make the food more interesting.

Quick short-cut cooking depends on this kind of imagination more than anything else; a subtle flavour and an attractive appearance make all the difference and is the mark of a clever, interested cook.

How to prepare
garNishEs aNd decoratioNs

Parsley Choose bright green parsley with tight curly leaves. Nip the curly heads off the stalks, wash in cold water and shake or pat dry in a tea towel. Curly tops may be snipped off and used as a garnish simply as sprigs, or the sprigs may be chopped. Gather the sprigs in a small bunch, place on a chopping board and use a sharp medium-sized kitchen knife without a serrated edge. To chop parsley correctly, use the heel of the knife, as opposed to the tip. Using the left hand, push the parsley under the heel of the knife while chopping with the right hand – this cuts the parsley coarsely.

For further fine chopping, hold the tip of the knife with the fingers of the left hand, keeping the tip of the knife on the board and chop using the right hand, swinging the knife back and forwards over the parsley, chopping until fine enough. Parsley is best stored unchopped if kept for any length of time.

To use Parsley sprigs look pretty tucked in between stacks of sandwiches, placed on the top of shellfish cocktails, or as a garnish for open sandwiches or prepared meat dishes. Sprinkle chopped parsley over scrambled egg, buttered vegetables, especially carrots and new potatoes, or vegetables in a white sauce such as onions, cauliflowers or leeks. Sprinkle over fried fish, or over mixed grills, pork or lamb chops. Parsley also looks pretty on potato salad or simple hors d'oeuvre, such as sardines, tomato slices or hard-boiled eggs.

Tomato Choose firm, ripe tomatoes. Unripe tomatoes are difficult to peel; soft ones are difficult to cut. Skins from tomatoes may be removed if liked before using. Simply nick the skins of the tomatoes with a sharp knife on the rounded side, plunge into boiling water for 1 minute and then drain. Peel off the skins – where the tomato was nicked the skin will already have begun to curl up.

Tomato slices make a simple and effective garnish. Slice tomatoes cleanly either using a

very sharp steel kitchen knife or a serrated knife such as a bread knife. Place tomato stalk end to the table surface and slice downwards. Keep the slices in the correct order so they retain the tomato shape and lay flat. Alternatively, tomatoes may first be cut in half, then into quarters. Dip the centre edge in finely grated Parmesan cheese, or finely chopped parsley.

Tomato lilies are cut using a small, sharp-pointed kitchen knife. Hold the tomato in the left hand and with the knife in the right hand push the knife tip into the centre of the tomato at an angle. Work round the centre of the tomato placing the knife at opposite angles for each cut, taking care to hit the tomato centre each time. When completed, lift the two halves apart and place a small sprig of parsley in each centre.

To use Sliced tomatoes look marvellous on open sandwiches, to garnish grilled hamburgers, over potato topping on shepherd's pie and on baked or grilled fish. Cut into wedges, or use tomato lilies to garnish salads, plates of sandwiches or cold meats.

Cucumber Cucumber can be peeled or left unpeeled and then sliced at an angle. Garnish slices with a thin slice of stuffed olive or a sprig of parsley in the centre. Try alternating slices of cucumber and tomato in a row and garnish with chopped parsley. Try placing cucumber slices over a slice of lemon, cut through both with a sharp knife from the outer edge to the centre only. Turn the edges inwards, overlapping to make a cone, and place a sprig of parsley in the cone. Or, twist the edges in opposite directions to make a cucumber and lemon twist.

Keep a cucumber stalk end downwards in a glass of water — cover the cut end with cling film or kitchen foil.

To use Cucumber slices look fresh and crisp over cold fish or served with cold meats or ham. Arrange cones on open sandwiches, or around the edge of any plate along with snipped cress. Cucumber and lemon twists look dramatic on a crab or lobster salad, or fried fish dishes.

Lemon Lemons are ideal for garnishes and are very versatile. They may be cut across making pretty lemon slices — garnish the centre with a sliced stuffed olive or chopped parsley. Or cut the lemon lengthwise into wedges and dip the lemon centre edge in chopped parsley or paprika.

A lemon left plain may be sliced to make lemon butterflies. Cut plain slices in half, then cut each half to the centre into quarters but leave the centre segments attached. Gently open out and garnish with parsley sprigs. Lemon twists can be made cutting plain lemon slices into the centre then twist the two edges in opposite directions, add a sprig of parsley if liked.

Remember when cutting lemons to use a stainless steel knife as the acid in the fruit discolours steel knives and the lemon flesh, unless wiped between each slice.

To use Lemon goes best with fish dishes. Garnish fried fish with lemon butterflies or slices adding a little chopped parsley. Fix lemon slices on rims of glasses with shellfish cocktail. Serve lemon twists with veal or pork escalopes or veal blanquette or decorate shrimp or prawn open sandwiches. Lemon wedges go with potted prawns, smoked fish, or pancakes.

Paprika pepper Paprika pepper is a bright red colour and used in cookery mostly for the colour that it contributes. It should not be confused with cayenne pepper which is also bright red but has a very hot and pungent flavour.

The use of paprika pepper is limited; attractive lines of paprika pepper can be used as a garnish on egg slices or lemon wedges. Tip the pepper out on to a square of kitchen foil or greaseproof paper, then using a knife pick up evenly along the knife edge as much pepper as you wish to use. Tip quickly over the item to be garnished, making a straight even line. This procedure can be used with very finely chopped parsley and the two used together give a pretty contrast in colour. Pinches of paprika pepper are pretty for adding a colour contrast in otherwise plain food.

Paprika pepper comes in jars with shaker tops — store in a cool dry cupboard; once you buy a bottle it will last for months.

To use It makes a nice colour contrast sprinkled over vegetables in white sauce particularly cauliflower, or scrambled eggs, or over a creamy potato salad along with snipped chives. Lines of paprika look dramatic across egg mayonnaise.

Nuts Jars of nuts are invaluable for dessert decorations. Walnuts and almonds are the most useful. Walnuts may be used whole or chopped. Coarsely chop walnuts, using scissors, and snip them into pieces. For finely chopped walnuts, chop them in the same manner as parsley. Never mince walnuts; the pressure squeezes out the oil and the fine pieces stick together.

Almonds may be purchased in their skins, blanched or chopped; or as almond nibs or flakes — finely sliced. *To blanch almonds*, that is to remove the outer brown skin on whole almonds, plunge the almonds into boiling water for 1 minute. Drain and quickly pop the almonds out of the skins. While almonds are still warm, it's a good idea to chop or slice them. When cold and hardened they tend to break up more. *Toasted almonds* have a delicious flavour and look prettier than the untoasted ones. Spread almonds out on a baking tray or grill pan and

place under a high heat. Either way shake the almonds occasionally to get even colouring and don't leave them — they burn very quickly.

To use Chopped walnuts are nice sprinkled over any custard-based desserts, and over instant whips or ice cream. Flaked toasted almonds are delicious sprinkled over creamed rice desserts, canned pears, and are particularly nice with apricots, old-fashioned chocolate pudding, blancmange or apple snow.

Coconut Desiccated coconut being plain white lends itself ideally to added colouring for decoration. Spoon the required amount into a jar; unless specially required, don't do more than 2 tablespoons at a time. Add a few drops of any food colouring — it's best to use red, green or yellow. Cover with a lid, cap or piece of kitchen foil and shake vigorously to colour all the coconut evenly. Tip the coconut out on to a square of foil and leave in a warm place to dry before storing in the jar.

Toasted coconut is also effective; spread coconut over a square of kitchen foil in the base of a grill pan and toast, under a high heat, shaking until evenly browned.

To use Sprinkle over whipped cream toppings, particularly around edges of trifles or moulded milk puddings.

Chocolate Plain chocolate is more suitable than milk chocolate, the darker colour being more effective as a colour contrast. To get more striking shapes and texture, the chocolate should be melted and then used. Break the chocolate into a small mixing basin and set this over a pan of hot water — take care to select a basin that fits the pan neatly.

Heat the water in the pan until almost boiling then draw off the heat. Chocolate should never be melted over direct heat, nor should any water, even in the form of steam from the pan, be allowed to come in contact with it.

Chocolate has unusual properties, and its texture and shiny appearance can easily be spoiled. When melted, spread the chocolate on to a flat surface.

For *chocolate curls*, spread the chocolate thinly on marble or Formica and allow to cool but not set firm. Then choose a medium-to-large steel kitchen knife with a plain edge. Holding the knife tipped backwards at an angle, shave the chocolate into curls. As long as the knife is held at a sloping angle the chocolate will curl into long cigarette shapes. Pick out the best shapes and place separately; broken shavings can be kept in a box. Store covered in a cool place, preferably the refrigerator.

To use Chocolate curls look really attractive placed on top of chocolate gâteaux that are plain-iced with chocolate icing. Use also on top of chocolate cup cakes and sprinkled over the tops of creamy desserts or over ice cream.

Glacé fruits Glacé cherries and angelica are most suitable for decoration — other glacé fruit can be a little expensive. Glacé cherries are obtainable in green and gold colours as well. Before using any glacé fruit, always wash off the sticky preserving syrup with warm water. Cherries may be cut in halves, quarters or they can be finely chopped.

Angelica may also be chopped but it is best cut into angelica leaves. To make these, first cut the angelica into 5-mm to 1-cm/$\frac{1}{4}$- to $\frac{1}{2}$-inch strips. Then cut across at an angle to make diamond shapes. Arrange leaves and cherries together to make pretty designs.

To use Glacé cherry halves can be placed in the centre of prepared grapefruit halves or in melon wedges. Chopped glacé fruits look pretty stirred into canned fruit, particularly pears or peaches. Decorate meringue toppings on lemon pie or queen of puddings with angelica and cherries. Arrange pretty designs of both in the bases of jelly desserts so when turned out they appear on the top.

Index